Quick and Easy, Proven Recipes

Cooking on a Budget

Publisher's Note: Raw or semi-cooked eggs should not be consumed by babies, toddlers, pregnant or breastfeeding women, the elderly or those suffering from a chronic illness.

Publisher & Creative Director: Nick Wells
Senior Project Editor: Catherine Taylor
Editorial: Esme Chapman
Art Director: Mike Spender
Layout Design: Jane Ashley
Digital Design & Production: Chris Herbert

Non-recipe text: Simoney Girard

Special thanks to Laura Bulbeck and Frances Bodiam.

This is a **FLAME TREE** Book

FLAME TREE PUBLISHING
Crabtree Hall, Crabtree Lane
Fulham, London SW6 6TY
United Kingdom
www.flametreepublishing.com

First published 2014

14 16 18 17 15
1 3 5 7 9 10 8 6 4 2

ISBN: 978-1-78361-300-7

A copy of the CIP data for this book is available from the British Library.

Printed in Singapore

All images are courtesy of Flame Tree Publishing Limited except the following which are courtesy of **Shutterstock.com** and © the following contributors: 6 Robert Kneschke; 7b BlueOrange Studio; 7t Foodpictures; 10 Kellis; 11 mangostock; 18 wawritto; 23 Charles Amundson; 28 Dmitriy Shironosov; 29 Richard Pratt; 31 Mona Makela; 32 LeonP; 34 catlook; 37 Lepas; 38 tacar; 41 Ildi Papp; 45 Audi Dela Cruz; 47 Olga Miltsova; 48 PhotoSGH; 49 Janis Smits; 52 Vitaly Korovin; 53 Bombaert Patrick; 54 sarsmis; 58 Mert Toker; 59 nicobatista; 60 gnohz; 61 bonchan; 62 MartinsL; 12b, 21b gpointstudio; 12t, 19, 20, 21t, 26, 33, 42b, 57t Monkey Business Images; 13b iofoto; 13t Iakov Filimonov; 14b, 15b, 25t, 27 Yuri Arcurs; 14t dotshock; 15t Juriah Mosin; 16, 35b Africa Studio; 17b micro10x; 17t igor kisselev; 22b Goran Bogicevic; 22t kuppa; 24b Pieter Stander; 24t, 43 Elena Elisseeva; 25b Jane Rix; 30, 51 Stephen Mcsweeny; 35t Ilya Andriyanov; 36b jabiru; 36t Aynia Brennan; 38b PeterKikta; 39t BW Folsom; 42t, 44b Joe Gough; 44t Digivic; 46b Paul Cowan; 46t fpolat69; 50, 55 Alena Brozova; 57b Joe Belanger; 63b Floydine; 63t stockcreations; 64b VikaRayu; 64t donatas1205; 65b grynold; 65t Gayvoronskaya_Yana.

Quick and Easy, Proven Recipes

Cooking on a Budget

**FLAME TREE
PUBLISHING**

Contents

Introduction

Even when we are not experiencing a massive global credit crunch, rising inflation, a reduction in lending or a squeeze on our spending and saving, shopping, planning and cooking on a tight budget is a constant challenge for millions of people. And yet, believe it or not, it is perfectly possible to cook tasty, healthy and filling dishes without breaking the bank.

The recipes in this book are all tailored to cost as little as possible, without scrimping on taste or quantity, but first and foremost, it is important to learn how to buy food cheaply, cook economically and avoid wastage. There are many tips and skills to discover, but it will soon become second nature to shop within the household budget without restricting yourself or your family to a limited, boring or unhealthy diet.

Lessons from Our Forebears

Thankfully, we are not in unfamiliar territory. There are millions of people alive today around the world who lived through the Great Depression, the Second World War and the post-war gloom. They had large families to feed, bills to pay and a tight budget on which to live. And they did survive, showing great resourcefulness in the way they shopped, grew their own, cooked and stored their food.

This book is not advocating a return to the 1940s, to a time of powdered eggs, reusing old teabags and borrowing a cup of sugar from your neighbour. What we are advocating is considering the resourcefulness of our forebears, who made the most of the little they had, and looking at ways to apply some of these handy hints and tips to our own individual situations.

For example, with a bit of practice, you need never buy any more stocks, soups, pastes or preserves because you can grow, cook, prepare and store them yourself. Even 50 years ago, it was considered a luxury to buy your soups or preserves. Recipes dredged up from the inter-war years and the Second World War celebrations show just how easy it really is to cook some of these things from scratch.

An Arsenal of Cost-saving Techniques

There are modern ways to make savings too. The internet has brought with it a host of opportunities at our fingertips: the ability to compare and contrast prices and discounts on offer at various supermarkets; information on how to grow and store our own fresh produce; and useful ideas to help us save electricity and gas when cooking a meal, for example.

So, there is no need to restrict yourself to low-cost, high-fat convenience food. Throw the ready meals out of the window and say hello to home-made meals that the whole household will enjoy – we can feed ourselves on what seems to be an ever-tightening household spend. Let this book be a motivation to stop worrying about where the money will come from, and start making great plans to provide great meals, no matter how tight the budget becomes.

Introduction

Essentials

This chapter will bring you up to speed on everything you need to know to cook delicious, filling and healthy meals without breaking the bank. Beginning with advice on how to set your initial budget, you will also learn how to plan an economical shop and how to make the most of tactics and offers. Also discover tips on stretching out meals and storing leftovers, as well as learning the key store-cupboard ingredients that any savvy shopper should always have in stock.

Setting the Budget

Your budget is not always going to be as simple as, say, £5 per meal – that does not include snacks or small meals, for example. Before setting out to go food shopping, it is important to set a budget that you will not excede – but it must be realistic. People often set unrealistically small targets, which can cause further monetary problems.

Working Out How Much You Can Spend

Obviously, this depends on your income, and how much is left over after paying off all those other bills: heating, energy, travel, rent or mortgage... Official research statistics prove that people, especially families, are finding it increasingly difficult to meet food costs: you are not alone if you are wondering how to make ends meet. But even assuming that there is a little left in the barrel after the mortgage and other bills are paid, you also have to be realistic about how much your shop comes to. How can you gauge what is essential expenditure?

Keep Your Till Receipts

By keeping till receipts, you can look back at, say, three months' worth of receipts and work out what the average spend should be. This can be important in setting your food budget for the year ahead. Here are some benefits of doing this:

∽ **Price rises** You can see which foodstuffs have risen in price. This will help you decide whether a different store might work out to be better value.

∽ **Not-so-little extras** You can see how much 'extra' and unplanned food items cost. This will help you stick to your shopping list (*see* 'Planning the Shop', page 16) and avoid shelling out for items you did not consider in the budget plan.

∽ **What do you not eat?** Looking at the receipts, are there any food items you buy that you do not really eat? Have you just got into the habit of buying three bottles of milk a week, when in fact you only really need two?

∽ **The average spend** Shopping bills can help you work out an average spend and can help you think about keeping within a certain band. By cutting out the unnecessary and the unplanned, you could set a reasonable budget, setting an upper and lower limit for flexibility, for each week. You will save money immediately if you stick within that band.

∽ **Checking supermarkets** Comparing receipts from different stores will indicate where to shop for the best prices on your staples such as cereal, bread, juice and meat. It is not just about comparing random prices across each store to see who has got the highest number of discounts, but looking at what you actually buy and whether this research can help lower your budget.

Setting the Budget

Think Ahead for Special Occasions

If you know you have a birthday or celebration coming up, make sure you factor this extra expenditure into your budget. Either set up a separate cash account way in advance to save for this expenditure, or make a sensible budget plan for that week's food spend.

Spend As Much As You Eat

No more, no less! Do not cut back so much that meals are insufficient, but do not overestimate what you or your family can eat. A filling, healthy meal can be provided within a sensible budget.

Waste Not, Want Not

If you overestimate the spend, you will be tempted to use up the full amount, probably on overpriced snack foods or stuff that will only get thrown away. Even in 2008, according to the World Food Programme, consumers in the US, UK and Western Europe were wasting 30 per cent of food purchased. In the US alone, this was worth an estimated US$48.3bn.

Ways Not to Waste

Thinking about what tends to get wasted in your household will help you work out what to buy and what not to buy. Here are some things to help you get started:

- **Forgotten fridge items** What tends to get left in the fridge until it has curdled its way past its use-by date? Yogurts? Pickles? Cut back on buying it.

- **Timing is everything** Does your household tend to eat more at lunchtime (away from home) and only want a little to eat in the evening? Then do not buy loads of ingredients for big evening meals, as these are likely to linger until they are thrown out.

- **Only buy what you want** Buying more than you need means too much waste food at the end of the week.

- **Bake it, don't fake it** Do you buy several cakes (on the insistence of your eight-year-old) that get only half-eaten? Why not just buy the bare ingredients for baking a cake? It will save money in the long term and provide something fun to do together as a family or with friends.

Weekly or Monthly Budget?

Those who get paid weekly, or who do not own a car, may find that a smaller, weekly shop is better. In this case, work out how much you can set aside each week for spending, and apportion some of that to the food shop. There are two main advantages of weekly rather than monthly shopping:

- **Reducing waste** You will naturally reduce wastage, as you are more likely to use up all the food that you have bought; people who shop monthly often leave food to go past its use-by date.

Setting the Budget

∾ Cash is king Weekly shoppers may be more likely to use cash to pay for their groceries, so this keeps them within their set budget; it is easy to go overboard when you are carrying around a credit or debit card.

Card Caution

If you shop monthly, you are less likely to carry around a significant wad of cash in your wallet and are more likely to pay by card. This can be risky. Make sure that you are not tempted to bust your budget because you have the 'freedom' to do so on your credit or debit card. By the same token, avoid buying too much food that will only get wasted simply because you can. In both instances, the point is to stick within a reasonable, achievable budget and to see where you can shave off unnecessary expenses.

Where Do Your Priorities Lie?

It may be very difficult for you to make a regular budget. Perhaps you are self-employed or working on a contract-only basis, or you have debt problems. If there is only a certain amount left in the kitty and your average monthly shop is at least four times that amount, you either try to make do on what you have (which might be an unrealistic expectation if you have a big family, for example) or you sort out what other expenditures you have been laying out that require attention. You have to eat to live.

Ask Yourself How to Prioritise

By taking time to go through your finances at the start of the month, you will find you can set aside the right amount to cover important costs, such as the food budget, without getting further into debt or cutting back so far that you end up with beans for supper every night.

- **Eat out less** Perhaps you could go out less and put more food on the table?

- **Rearrange or pay off your loans** Do you need to sort out your loan arrangements so that you do not have to shell out such high rates of interest on repayments?

Who Can Help with Financial Planning?

In these recessionary times many people are finding they have to make less money go further. Sometimes this can be particularly difficult, it is important to get some specialist advice to help out if you are really struggling. Possible sources of help are:

- **Bank** A personal representative at your bank should be able to give you some free budgeting advice.

- **Independent financial adviser** If you pay a fee, as opposed to commission, you should get completely impartial advice on your situation. The internet offers various ways of searching for a qualified adviser in your area.

- **Your accountant** If you have your own accountant, make use of them!

- **A debt specialist** You can contact a debt specialist at a free, charity-based service such as Mind or the Citizens Advice Bureau.

Setting the Budget

Planning the Shop

٤

So, you have your budget sorted out and decided whether you tend to shop monthly or weekly. Now it comes to planning ahead. This is the best way to save money and stick within your budget – and it really takes no time at all! We are not talking about a military-style attitude towards meals, but taking a couple of minutes to think ahead about what you need could save you a lot of money.

Making a List

Making a list is really important. How many times have you come back from the supermarket without the toilet rolls or washing-up liquid? How many times have you, instead, bought six or seven items that you did not need, just because you were not sure whether you needed them or not?

Tips for Compiling

Instead of rushing at the last minute to make a list of things you need to get, or not bothering at all and picking up anything you see, try the following:

∾ **The till receipts** Use your last few shopping bills as a basis for remembering certain items and working out which supermarkets could offer the best price on the essentials.

∾ **Who ate the last cookie?** Take note of 'empties' during the week. Why not keep a magnetic notepad on the fridge and train yourself (and your family) to write down when they finish an item?

- **Running on empty** Make a note of everyday items that are running low, especially those items which might not be as widely available in many supermarkets. These might be things such as special soya milk or gluten-free bread.

- **Keep the coupons handy** If you have particular money-off coupons, or have saved up loyalty points or stamps, make sure that you keep these with the list, in your wallet or purse, ready for the big shop.

Branded for Life

How many times have you or a family member bought the wrong brand or flavour of something, only for it to sit on the shelf until it gets thrown away? Keeping a list can also help you remember which brand and type of food went down well with everyone, and which brands were met with general disapproval. This will help reduce unnecessary spending and keep your household budget low.

Planning the Weekly Meals

If you have a rough plan in your head for what the week has in store in terms of meals, you will save money by being able to include the appropriate components in your list. This is because you will have what you need and will not have to rush out at the last-minute to a more expensive local or convenience store; you can gauge quantities more precisely, so you do not end up buying more than you need; you can figure out where to go for the best deals on certain food items you need for various meals; and, if you are going to have guests over for dinner one night, you can think ahead to make the most of any bargains or bulk-buy discounts.

Planning the Shop

When to Shop?

༄

We all lead busy lives, so it is no wonder that the majority of us pile down to the nearest supermarket on a Saturday or Sunday in order to get in the weekly or monthly groceries. But this can lead to a quick dash round a crowded supermarket, with fractious children and hungry teenagers loitering wistfully around the freshly-baked cookies counter. Being stressed leads to the famous phrase: 'Let's just get out of here as quickly as possible', which can lead to picking up the first thing you see, rather than having the time to compare prices or search for the best bargains.

The Early Bird Catches the Worm

Why not get up a little earlier and shop when there are fewer people around and a clearer car park? You will have more leisure to follow your list and pick up more bargains along the way.

Evening Advantages

Or, if you can shop later on in the evening, and especially on a weekday, you will not only find that it is not so crowded and you have time to think, but you will also find that many supermarkets do discounts on big-ticket items towards the end of the day. And individual stores will set their own end-of-line bargain prices, which you will not see if you go online to compare stores. But remember, cheap does not mean necessary: do not be misled into thinking that because it is a 'bargain', you must need it. If it is not on the list, do not buy it.

Where to Shop?

In a busy world where we are cash-strapped and time-poor, it is difficult to make the right choices about where to shop. The local convenience store may be nearby and open all hours, but it probably costs significantly more than the supermarket that is 20 minutes' drive away. However, for some people, if they live far from the supermarket and do not have a car, or work unsociable hours, for instance, the convenience store can be the easiest and default option. But are there other options, and how do you tell who has the best bargains?

Online Shopping

Shops are also recognising that many people do not have the ability or time to do big weekly or monthly shops in store. Many supermarkets now offer online shopping, complete with door-to-door delivery, which can benefit you if you are unable to get to the shops physically, do not have the time to go or are likely to spend as much on petrol as on delivery.

User-friendly

Busy mother-of-two Misha Sergeant, from Leicester, says, 'When I'm just not able to get out to the shops, I find that internet shopping is quite a good way of making sure you only get what you need. As you look at the various items in your virtual basket, you can review the list and add on anything you have forgotten. Also, I have often got up, looked in my fridge and cupboards to see what I needed, then gone back to the computer and added these to the basket... and taken away things I didn't really need.'

Ask If There Are Any Discounts

Many of these delivery sites will have special delivery discounts and concessions for those who are elderly or have a disability, while others will offer 'extras' to boost online ordering.

Price Comparison on the Internet

A quick search for 'best prices for food shopping' will throw up a host of comparison websites, useful chat forums and even blogs that can help you compare prices. Some websites have updates to let you know which stores have recently discounted certain ranges and which stores are offering the best prices on certain foodstuffs, so you can get a pretty good picture of where you might be able to save money. Some sites claim that you can save between 20 and 30 per cent on your average family food shop. So, even if you do not intend to buy online, the internet can help you save money on your shop.

Price Comparison Websites

There are some websites, such as www.mysupermarket.co.uk, that enable you to automatically compare specific food prices in competing superstores. Some food shopping price comparison websites take you all the way through to purchasing your items, so you don't have to go to the actual store's website separately.

Earn Points and Find the Best Prices

Some price comparison sites have a loyalty scheme where you can gain virtual points with them as well as the usual points you will get with your specific supermarket on your store loyalty or club card. These virtual points can be traded at other sites for a variety of goods, days out or gifts. Also, some websites will show daily deals and best prices on a range of products at each supermarket. So, regardless of whether you want to swap supermarkets or not, you can see at a glance where the best prices are.

Deals of the Week

Each supermarket will feature its latest deals on its own website, whether weekly or daily. It is worth taking a peek at your store's website before you go shopping; if you have time, look at the nearest rival's website too, to see just what is on offer.

Discount Stores

The well-established brand-name superstores are facing stiff – and increasingly public – competition from non-domestic, self-proclaimed 'hypermarkets' such as Aldi, Lidl and Netto, who offer significant discounts in comparison to the big-name rivals. While other food giants are cutting jobs and closing stores, these newer discount stores are growing in popularity. They are able to do this through a mixture of bulk buying, low overheads through less attractive stores, not giving free bags, fewer staff and cutting it finer when it comes to use-by dates.

Are They Really Always Cheaper?

There are many surveys online that can help to gauge whether or not these stores really do offer better value for money. This is based not just on the number of food items sold at a lower price, but also the quality and the quantity (for example, whether the bulk buys offer a better saving in a cheaper outlet than a no-name or own-brand bulk buy in a 'domestic' store). A simple Google search will throw up some of these websites.

Which Foods Are Cheaper in These Stores?

The answer may be 'pretty much everything'. Food that is generally cheaper than in a standard supermarket includes:

Where to Shop

- Meat
- Cheese (significantly so)
- Bulk-buy pastas, noodles, rice
- Loose vegetables (check the freshness, though)
- Snack foods
- Frozen 'finger food' for parties
- Traditional Christmas or other seasonal food
- Cartons of fruit juice
- Cans of fruit or pie and pastry filling
- Four- and six-pack cans of soup, beans or pasta shapes (half the price)

Open Your Mind

Do not be put off by the fact that labels may be primarily in Spanish, German or Polish – most have translations into English. Many of these discounted items are leading brands in Mexico, Germany or Spain, similar to the leading brands in 'domestic' stores. Do not assume that it cannot be any good because it is an unfamiliar brand. You may find that it tastes better and is even healthier.

The Farmers' Market

These are more popular in rural areas, but are starting to make inroads into the cities thanks to the rising popularity of organic and free-range food. Markets are sometimes bypassed in this busy age of instant consumerism, but the experience is great, as is the potential for best-price bargains on fresh and home-made food. With a little careful planning, you can find out where the local markets are each week or month, and perhaps going to a farmers' market might become a nice day out once a month.

What Can You Get?

Although you cannot get a lot of the items you may buy in bulk from the supermarkets, such as cans and other non-perishables, there is still a wide range of produce available from farmers' markets (not to mention non-food items such as crafts), including fresh meat and meat produce, cheeses, sauces, pickles, syrups and jams, home-made wines and cordials, bread, cakes and pastries, home-grown vegetables and fruit, and dairy produce.

Are They Cheaper?

A farmers' market is not always cheaper, but they offer a different choice of produce to supermarkets, and more organic and ethically produced foods. And there are some savings to be had at farmers' markets:

- ❧ **Organic savings** Superstores usually charge higher prices for organic meat than you would pay for the same quality at a farmers' market.

- ❧ **Try before you buy** You can taste before you buy, which means that, if you do not like it, you do not have to buy it, unlike a supermarket where you have to buy first and thus risk wasting food.

- ❧ **Negotiation** Many of the farmers will do deals or haggle a price with you for bulk buys, so do not go by price tags alone.

The Traditional Market

Because many of these stallholders will import their food directly, they are not subject to the same tax restrictions as the supermarkets are. Plus, they want to sell off their goods at the end of the day because they do not have the storage – so competing cheaply on volume is the way to do it. Finally, the overheads a market trader will have to pay are very low compared with the bills a store has to face.

Where to Shop

Different Tastes

Immigration has done a wonderful thing in injecting new life into the flagging marketplaces of cities. It has brought new tastes and food ideas to the fore and has found a willing audience of people wanting to try new things without having to pay the higher prices that a supermarket will front-load onto the goods.

Fruit and Veg

There are several advantages at markets when it comes to fruit and vegetables:

- **By weight, not unit** Because market stalls charge according to weight, you will save money by getting just the right portions needed, without wasting any.

- **Exotic competition** Some exotic fruits, such as mangoes, pineapples, yams and plantains are far cheaper in markets or local grocery stores than in supermarkets.

- **You do not pay for packaging** Try this challenge – buy a packet of tomatoes from a supermarket and the same number of fresh ones loose from a market stall. The market stall's local produce will usually work out to be the best price for (usually) fresher goods.

- **Organic food** Luckily you will not pay supermarket prices for buying fresh, home-grown, organic produce from a local marketplace.

Fishmongers and Butchers

Sometimes it is best to cut out the middleman and go straight to the wholesalers. Superstores do not offer you the full range of meat cuts or always show you the best fish dishes to fit your budget. Many people wrongly assume that a butcher or fishmonger is going to be more expensive, as you pay a premium for the freshest meat, or that, because he is a smallholding, his higher overheads will be passed on to you. However, you could save a significant amount by learning how to cook some of the more unusual cuts available at butchers and also learn how to make your meals more varied, healthy and exciting.

A Meaty Difference

While supermarket-bought meat is convenient and cleanly packed, there are certain things to watch out for with meat in supermarkets:

- The 'water' load Many shops will inject water into meat to help it freeze. So, when they weigh meat, some stores will not take into account the water load and will charge you for both the meat and the water therein. The water, of course, evaporates in the cooking process, meaning you actually got less for your money.

- Actual weight v. price Also, while on the subject of weight, bear in mind that many weight-based prices fluctuate significantly on products such as cheese or meat, but the actual difference in terms of what you get to serve up on your plate is not always as great as the price may lead you to believe. For example, a pack of eight lamb chops might vary 'by weight' by as much as 50p. But will that variation make a difference to what your family will eat? Probably not – so get the cheaper option.

Where to Shop

- **Variety** A wholesale butcher or fishmonger at a market, or a local butcher's store, will have a wider range of cuts and often offer lower prices. A supermarket, because of space constraints, might not always devote shelf space to a wider (and potentially cheaper) range of cuts.

- **In-house butchers** Even if you do go to the butcher's counter at a supermarket, remember that, while you are getting fresh, quality-assured meat and a slightly wider range of cuts (for example, you will get liver and kidneys here), he is still there to raise money for the superstore and may not always offer you the cheapest cut each time.

Specialist Stores

Most supermarkets offer food from around the world to cater for increasingly diverse tastes. But there are also many independent shops and delicatessens that can offer more choice for your money. Just because they look specialist does not mean that they will charge you specialist prices. They are worth a look.

General Stores

Sometimes it is worth buying on impulse when it comes to looking for savings. General stores such as Poundland, The Pound Shop or 99p Stores, to name just a few, may not primarily be food stores, as they stock all sorts of products, but they may be the source of some surprise deals. If you see a deal in an unexpected place, for items you usually buy, then it is worth picking up the deal and crossing it off the shopping list. Just remember not to be fooled by the bright stickers stating that everything in the store is £1 – sometimes the foodstuff is cheaper in supermarkets. Quality-wise too, some of the no-brand cheap chocolates, wines and champagnes are not worth buying. Not everything is a best buy just because it is in a 'cheap' store.

Tactics and Offers

ℰ

There are all sorts of ways to improve your chances of getting the best deals when food shopping. There are so many kinds of offers or discounts and there are many pitfalls to be wary of. By doing all you can to shop wisely, you will find the best bargains and meet your budget.

Reduced to Clear

Most leading supermarkets will have a range of heavily discounted foodstuffs that are approaching the end of their shelf life. It is also worth asking if you might have a discount on damaged goods. However, remember the difference between the dates on produce: a 'use-by' date really means it is the end of a product's life, a 'best-before' date is a guideline (sometimes a foodstuff is good for a week after the best-before date) and a 'sell-by date' is an arbitrary measure telling staff when to replenish stock on the shelves (although the food may be good for a week or so yet).

Special Offers

There are all sorts of special deals around: 'buy-one-get-one-free' ('BOGOF') or 'two-for-one' ('2-4-1'), '25 per cent off (or extra)', 'three-for-the-price-of-two' and special half-price lures are becoming a mainstay in supermarkets throughout the year. This sort of deal is great if you really need what is being offered. It is worth planning this strategically, but do not get carried away. Overleaf are some pointers on how to treat special offers.

Look for Deals on the Staples

If you have the freezer space and you see deals on milk, bread, sausages, bacon and so on, then buy them and save them. This is particularly good for meat and higher-ticket items.

Be Alert

However, there are some things to watch out for, as not every deal may be the best bargain-buy for your family. There have been investigations by various consumer watchdogs about deals such as 2-4-1. They discovered that, while the special offer price takes into account the fact that two items are being sold for the price of one, the price of 'one' is somewhat nominal and has been found to have been raised when used as part of a buy-one-get-one-free deal. While the cost per item is proportionately cheaper than if bought on its own, it is not actually half price, critics claim. So be canny about your purchases.

Extra Free?

Offers of 25 per cent (or 50 per cent) 'extra' free have also generated flurries of customer letters claiming that stores and manufacturers sometimes put up the price of a product before coming out with a short-term '25 per cent extra free' offer. Other consumer champions have seen that the packaging may look a lot larger to entice consumers but, weight-for-weight, another similar product may be offering a better price.

Watch Your Budget

Finally, just because it is a special deal, if it is not on your usual shopping list, do not buy it. It will only break the food budget – show willpower!

Own Brands and Basics Brands

Many people like to stick to their well-known brands of pizza or pasta, whether out of habit or because of certain allergies or intolerances. However, leaving aside those who need to use certain brands because of health issues, breaking the habit of always buying the most expensive brand-name goods can save you a lot of money on your household shopping budget. There is an increasingly wide range of own-brand and no-brand, or 'basics', goods: you can get everything from pasta and margarine to feminine care and toothpaste. Look around for where the deals are to be found. You will be surprised at how much you can get for a lot less when you start to switch from the big-name brands to your store's own brand.

Busting the Brand Myth

Here are a few more pointers to encourage you to save money on your average food spend:

- **Read the ingredients** The reason why most products from your local store taste similar to leading brands should become obvious from reading the list of ingredients. They are nearly always the same, in more or less the same quantities.

- **Taste testing** When eggs, flour, raisins or butter from a store's own-brand range of food is mixed together into a cake, it is very hard for anyone to tell the difference between the own-brand ingredients and the leading brand names.

- **Fruit and vegetables** Sometimes there are ranges of packaged fruit and vegetables: a premium brand, the store's own brand and its basic or value-brand fruit or vegetables. There is little difference in the taste, particularly when cooked in a casserole.

Beware of the 'Budget Blinkers'

Do not get so caught up in buying the basics or value, no-frills range that you miss out on good offers on branded goods. Also, try not to let your mission for the cheapest food obscure any ethical considerations – for example, buying free-range eggs instead of eggs from battery or caged hens.

Making the Most of Deals and Offers

In addition to the 2-4-1s, do not forget to get as much as you can out of coupons, points and other deals, as well as your loyalty cards.

Junk Mail

Do not throw away any marketing that comes through your door before you have checked it. There may be some discount coupons that will be useful. Keep them in your wallet.

Look Online

Sometimes money-off vouchers can be found on independent websites or the store's own website. You can print these off and use them against certain items. Beware, though; not all the vouchers may be for everyone to use. The same applies to discount delivery codes, which are internet codes that can cut the price of home shopping.

Take a Raincheck

Ask for what are commonly called 'raincheck' vouchers – if a special offer item is not in stock, the store manager might give you a voucher entitling you to the same deal at a later date.

Points Promotions

In-store deals offering extra points for a particular product are a great way to save for that rainy day or big celebration.

Surveys

If you are offered the chance to win free shopping for a year just by filling in a survey, then go for it. What have you got to lose? Or, rather, what could you gain?

Making the Most of Your Loyalty Cards

You are earning points, so make the most of them by spending them to defray the cost of your shopping every now and then. If you can collect Air Miles on these cards, even better – your food shopping could help to pay for your holiday to Florida.

Starting to Cook

۲

With most of us having busy working lives, it is a chore to think about cooking a meal every night. It is no surprise that many people opt for a takeaway, ready meal or the convenience store for their nightly dinner. Plus, if you have a family to cook for, this can be even more difficult: with many families working on shift patterns, teenagers out or hibernating in their rooms for much of the evening, planning and preparing the meal can be almost impossible. Almost, but not quite.

Working out Quantities

Whether you are cooking for one or five, working out quantities can be tricky. With a family, even assuming that everyone in the house likes and can eat the same food (which would be a miracle), the sheer quantities of food involved can be mind-boggling.

Cooking with Bulk Items
Having saved money by buying family-size packs or bulk items such as noodles, frozen peas or rice, it is sometimes tempting to use a little more of these than we should in each meal, because the bag or packet looks never-ending. Here is a secret – it is not. It will run out sooner than you think, unless you are careful.

Don't Just Use It Up
If you think there is only a little bit of a certain ingredient left, you might be tempted to throw it all in. Don't. It will only get wasted. Try making it into something, such as a soup or stuffing.

Never Overestimate

Too often we are not convinced that a certain amount of food will be enough per person. But think about the various appetites: small children and older people will not eat huge portions. Try the following:

- ∾ Measure it out! Until you get used to cooking a certain dish so that you can automatically gauge the right amount, use measuring cups, scales and jugs to help you get the right portion per person.

- ∾ Make a fist This should be the size of a portion of noodles, mashed potato or rice to accompany a meal for an adult.

- ∾ Count the carrots Assume, as a rough rule of thumb, that half a carrot should be apportioned per person as part of a wider meal. Apply the same rule to parsnips, celery, courgettes and aubergines.

- ∾ Divvy up the potatoes When doing roasts, count the prepared potatoes in the pan and allocate a certain even number to each person (usually between four and six). Someone will always want more or less, so it balances out.

Working from Recipes

This is the easiest way to gauge how much food you will need to prepare per person. Recipes enable you to:

- ∾ Plan the shop Do you need more chicken than you have in the freezer, for instance?

- ∾ Conduct mental swaps Work out what to replace certain ingredients with so that you can use what you have, rather than buy new things.

- ∾ Think about portion allocation Estimate how much each family member can eat.

- **Think about leftovers** You will be able to gauge whether you will have enough left over for someone's lunch the next day.

- **Trial and Error** If you are not working from a recipe, or the recipe resulted in too much or too little, you will learn from trial and error. If you have not baked enough lasagne one day, for example, make a note of it and increase the amounts you use the next time. If you have made too much food, write down what tends to get half-eaten or left on plates and cook less of it next time.

Time Matters

It is no wonder people grab a takeaway, open a ready-made pasta packet or bung a ready meal into the microwave. We live in a fast-paced world and while we might enjoy cooking when we have the chance, we often find ourselves pressed for time: work, family and other commitments all crowd in. But it is possible to stop buying the convenience food and the ready-made sauces and start saving money while not adding to our stress levels.

The Kitchen Time Lord

If you cook for other people or have a family, each person may need to eat at different times. Students eating at weird hours of the day, working adults coming home late and children leaving school early and demanding to be fed immediately: all these can take the stuffing out of the person preparing the food. And if we are not careful, this will take the stuffing out of our budget as well. So try not to keep people waiting too long for their meal or they will snack, but also remember to work in small stages so you do not have to do too many things at once.

A Step in Time

Knowing in advance when people will get up and come back home is a starting point. Of course, this involves communication, but preparing home-cooked meals and snacks will save lots of money, helping everyone not to rely on takeaways or quick-fix ready meals, while getting them involved, however old they are.

Stretching Meals

༕

There is a lot to be said for leftovers! And meals can go further than you think. This section looks more in depth at how to make a meal out of just a few ingredients, using leftovers in resourceful ways, avoiding wastage and making your own so you do not have to spend lots of money buying items such as sauces and stocks.

Making a Meal Go Further

If you are running low on ingredients, there is no need to rush for the nearest store to stock up. Take a look around at what you do have first, as this will save you time and money.

Thicken it Up!

If you are cooking a casserole or stew, but do not think there is enough meat or prime ingredient to go round, thicken it up with peas, lentils, rice, sweetcorn, potatoes or pasta shapes.

Short on Vegetables...

If you do not have enough vegetables to accompany a meal, instead of buying new ones, think about making them up into a 'sauce' by adding a little stock and ketchup, some chopped tomatoes or some tomato soup.

Long on Staples?

Do not just add more staple food to the plate to make it look like there is more food! Think about how to make it more interesting – it could be as simple as adding caraway seeds and black beans to rice, or mashing onion, mustard or leftover broccoli into mashed potatoes.

Be Bold

Be willing to try adding new or different ingredients, but please account for tastes:

- **Low on minced beef?** Try bulking up your Bolognese sauce with a little sausage, chopped ham or grated carrot.

- **Running low on cheese?** Make a herby white sauce to cover the cauliflower or macaroni, and then grate the small piece of cheese on top of the dish before cooking.

- **Thicken soups** Add puréed potato (boil it up and blend it to a pulp) to soups and broths to thicken them.

- **Oaty crumble topping** Mix oats and flour to create crumble toppings if you are low on flour.

- **Improve pizzas** Jazz up plain pizzas with leftover pepper, tomatoes and sweetcorn.

New Dishes from Leftovers

You can always find ways to use those 'little bits' left over for the whole family to enjoy, rather than have one person eating them up or, worse, throwing them away. Waste not, want not... Here are some examples:

Bubble and Squeak

A classic for brunch or a light dinner, this uses odds and ends of potato, vegetables and meat, all bound together with egg and fried (you can use low-fat oil instead of the traditional lard!). All the ingredients, except for the

egg, should have been cooked beforehand. Simply dice the cold meat and vegetables, beat the eggs (allowing one egg per person) and then stir them into the meat and vegetables. Fry over a moderate heat for 10–15 minutes, turning after 5 minutes.

Rissoles

Another wartime classic, rissoles are a brilliant way of using leftovers without making your family groan with boredom. These can be made using any leftover cooked meat or vegetables, and will stretch a small amount of food. Simply dice the meat or veg and reserve, then, in a pan, make a white sauce from any leftover gravy or stock (made up with 300 ml/½ pint milk), some seasoning and 1 heaped tablespoon flour. After it boils, add the meat or veg, spread it onto a plate, cool it down and add breadcrumbs. Shape it how you like, let it set for a while, then fry it up.

Meat Paste

This was popular in the interwar period during the 1920s and 1930s, and was used on toast, or as a cheap pâté with cheese, crackers and quince. Simply take the remainder of any cooked meat, mince it finely, add some herbs and spices and push through a sieve. Mix it together with 50 g/2 oz butter and put it into jars, pouring a little melted butter over the top to seal in the flavour.

Vegetable or Meat Timbales

Made using leftover minced meat, canned ham or corn, or roast vegetables, timbales are very similar to rissoles, only they are steamed instead of being fried. Blend the leftover meat or vegetables together with 25 g/1 oz breadcrumbs, 1 egg and some herbs. Make up a white sauce (see page 47 for instructions) and mix this into the ingredients along with salt and pepper. Pour the mixture into greased moulds and steam for 20–30 minutes. Timbales are delicious served with a small helping of plain pasta, lightly tossed with oil and parsley.

Multiple Remixes

There are so many ways to make each of the dishes above, and there are many more dinners that can be made out of what is left over. The objective of the cooks of yesteryear, who came up with the idea of turning one day's meal into another completely different one, was to prevent boredom as much as to protect the food budget. People rarely want to eat the same thing two days in a row; with careful planning and a little bit of panache, easy dishes can stretch the leftover food into a delicious meal the following day without stretching your bank account.

One Day's Dinner is the Next Day's Lunch

Well, not necessarily the next day – you have the option of storing and saving it for a day or so later, for when you feel like it. But however you want to mix it up for variety, the fact remains that if you use leftovers wisely, you will save a lot of money by not having to spend on expensive lunches. Even if you would 'only' spend a few pounds on lunch each day, if you do it every day for five days, this works out at quite a significant potential saving in the working week. Multiply that by 52 and you could knock a staggering sum off your yearly food budget.

Bake and Freeze

By making a little more than you would eat one day, you can save the remaining food for another. For example, suppose you bake a lasagne for six people, accompanied with salad or vegetables, but you are a family of four. You might have enough for two whole adult portions left over, which you could freeze together or separately. This could become two days' worth of lunch, or a light meal another evening.

Stretching Meals

The Cold Roast Sandwich

Everyone knows the famous turkey sandwich, made the day after Christmas with the leftover turkey meat and stuffing. But why not apply this 'rule' to every roast meal that you have? Doing this means that you will not need to throw away the leftover cuts of meat if there were only a few remaining post-roast; nor will you have to store a small amount in the fridge or freezer. Most importantly, you will save money by avoiding lunchtime purchases and spending less on sandwich fillers.

Sad Salad

If you have had a salad the night before and there is only a dribble left, do not throw it out. It could be used in a sandwich, to garnish a baked potato, or bolstered up with a little more lettuce and chopped tomato and made into a light lunch the next day. Remember, the more you save, the less you need to buy – and the less you need to buy, the healthier your budget will be.

Soups, Stocks and Sauces

It is shocking when we consider how much we pay for shop-bought meat or pasta sauces, canned soups, condiments and stock. Yet all these things can be made really cheaply with the ingredients we already have – and are using without knowing it – when we cook. They are really easy as well, so why do we not do it more often instead of spending? Here are just a few ideas to help you make your own and cut out a significant portion of your household food budget.

Apple Sauce

Apples that are going a little, well, wrinkly, are no good to eat but they are good for sauces and cooking. Instead of throwing them out, wash, peel, chop and boil them up with a little sugar and water and you have ready-made chunky apple sauce that can be used in pies, crumbles, preserves and to accompany pork.

Resourceful Salad Dressings

Many people buy salad dressing that only gets used once or twice, then is left to go mouldy in the fridge drawer. This is a waste and will damage the budget. But it is possible to make your own while using up the odds and ends of other jars and bottles. You need: the last bit of Dijon mustard, the remnants of the vinegar bottle and a scoop of honey (or whatever is left in the old jar). Mix them all together with a little warm boiled water and you have a honey and mustard salad dressing.

White Sauce

Rather than buying expensive packet mixes or jars of white sauces, make them yourself by stirring a little flour into a saucepan with some melted butter and whisking in some milk, little by little, until it has all blended but not boiled. Stir continuously. This is a basic white sauce, to which you could add pepper, if liked. To make it béchamel sauce, add some grated nutmeg and a little cream, or to make it cheese sauce, add some grated cheese and some herbs. To save on milk, use milk diluted with vegetable water.

Cheat's Soup

If you have not got enough leftovers for a sufficient portion for another meal, or even for bubble and squeak or rissoles, make the leftovers into a soup with the addition of lentils to thicken it into a hearty broth. Serve with cheese on toast. See the Soups & Starters section for some ideas.

Pasta Sauce

This is great for lasagnes and uses up lots of bits of vegetables. If you have a sausage or piece of ham left over from a previous meal, chop this into tiny pieces, together with half a grated carrot and half a grated celery stalk. You do not need wine. Add half an onion, fry the

Stretching Meals

sausage or ham in a little oil, then add the onion and the rest of the grated vegetables. When they are starting to brown, add 150 g/5 oz minced beef (you can buy basic or no-frills for this) and, when this is browned, add a large tin of tomatoes and some dried herbs. You can simmer this on a low heat for 40 minutes, or in a slow cooker.

Vegetarian Spaghetti Bolognese Sauce

Chop up an old half or whole onion and brown in a frying pan in a little light cooking oil, then add a large tin of chopped tomatoes and any tomatoes that are looking a little overripe, some dried herbs and any bits of pepper or other vegetables that you have left in your fridge. Simmer and season with Worcestershire sauce (you may have to source vegetarian kinds online), or similar, to taste.

Make Your Own Stock

Stock is the liquid obtained when bones, meat, fish or vegetables have been simmered in water to extract the flavour. It is the basis of most soups, sauces, stews and gravies. So, instead of spending on packaged stock cubes or (worse) jars of sauce or gravy, make your own in typical 1930s style: the water in which meat, rice or vegetables have been boiled may be substituted for stock, so, if the household is large, a stockpot should be kept in the fridge, into which should be put all suitable scraps such as vegetable peelings, tomato skins, meat trimmings and leftover scraps – avoid starchy food such as potatoes, as this makes it cloudy. Boil it up, skim off any fat, strain and use. If you are keeping it for more than a day, boil it up each day.

Maximise the Meal, Minimise the Spend

Hopefully, this has given you more of an idea about how to use up the leftovers instead of resorting to throwing them out. It is not about using up the scraps left over on people's plates, but about what is left in the pots after serving up the right portions for each person, and making the most of the little bits and bobs in your fridge and cupboards to maximise your meals and minimise your spend. For more ideas, check out www.lovefoodhatewaste.com.

Set Yourself a Cost Target

❧

Supermarket chains and celebrity chefs will have you believe that it is possible to cook a meal for four for just tiny sums of money. But even if this can be done, can it include extras such as dessert? Does it have to be completely done from scratch? And can families buy food for the week and generate interesting meals each day, without resorting to the seemingly cheap yet very unhealthy option of opening a couple of pizza boxes?

The Simple Answer...

... is yes. It can include desserts (see the case study on the Appleyards at the end of this section), it does not always have to be done from scratch each time and it is not difficult to budget for a series of interesting meals that do not require a huge number of ingredients.

Versatile Ingredients

When buying and planning the meals, always think about food that can be used in several different ways. This will help you if you want to buy in bulk – how many dishes can you create using that one bulk packet of a certain food item? Thinking about the versatility of ingredients can really help you cut back on the number of different food items that you buy, which will reduce your budget significantly.

🦶 Set Yourself a Cost Target

Versatile Staples

If you have a range of basic staple ingredients, you can chop and change and be prepared to be as flexible as possible when faced with time and money limits. Staples can be used in the following ways:

- ∾ Rice In addition to using it as a plain accompaniment to curries or stews, you can cook kedgeree, risotto, paella, rice pudding and egg-fried rice, or use it in rissoles, stuffing, soups, stews and casseroles, or prepare it with fish or vegetables for a salad.

- ∾ Potatoes Mash them, boil them, fry them into chips, bake them into wedges, purée them to form the basis of a thick soup, cut into chunks for curries, casseroles and stews, roast them, make them into fishcakes, bubble and squeak, moussaka, shepherd's pie, fish pie, hash browns, potato salad or the standard baked potato.

- ∾ Noodles Use noodles in stir-fries and soups, as ramen-style noodles, egg-fried noodles, or plain noodles to accompany another dish.

- ∾ Pasta (shapes, not ravioli, cannelloni, tortellini or spaghetti) Eat pasta freshly cooked and tossed in a sauce or accompanying 'meat and two veg', or make macaroni cheese, macaroni milk pudding, pasta bakes or pasta salad, or put pasta in soups and stews (such as minestrone soup).

Versatile Meat

There is more to meat than a roast dinner or bangers and mash. We will come on to the different fresh meat cuts that you can get to suit every type of budget, but let us first look at ways of using variations on the meat theme, taking some of the cheapest available meat products:

- **Burger meat** Available in big freezer packs and often at a discount, it is tempting just to slap these between two slices of bread roll with some cheese and bacon. However, they can also be used to make stews, hearty soups, casseroles, patties and pies and pasta sauces (if cooked and broken up with some onion, herbs and chopped tomatoes).

- **Minced meat:** This can be used to make various bulk meals that can be stored and frozen for future use. Some of its uses include bubble and squeak, chilli con carne, lasagne, meatloaf, meatballs, pasta sauce, pies and patties, rissoles, shepherd's pie, cottage pie and meat timbales.

- **Tinned meat** This includes tinned ham, spam and that other staple from the Second World War, corned beef. Ways to use these include bubble and squeak, cold sandwiches, cold as part of a ploughman's lunch, hot sandwiches such as melts, shepherd's pie, pastries, rissoles, sliced into salads, in pasta dishes (tinned ham, cut into chunks) and in soups.

- **Sandwich** (sliced, packaged) meat This does not just have to be put into sandwiches. It can also be used in the following ways: in hot melts, added to pizza topping, eaten cold as part of a ploughman's or other light lunch, salads (sliced thinly), mixed into pasta dishes such as carbonara, pastries and croque monsieurs/madames.

- **Sausages** Delightful hot or cold, on their own or inside a roll or sandwich, they can also be used in a sausage and pepper casserole; cooked, sliced and added to beans; diced up in a lasagne; cut up into chunks and added to stews; served cold, sliced, with salad; or in pastries.

Fishy Tales

Whether you get your fish right from the wharf, out of a tin or a cut from the supermarket, you can cook it many ways. Some of these methods can create a big quantity of food for a small amount

of money. These dishes can then be put into the freezer to save for another day. Ways to cook or use fish (tinned, frozen or fresh) include: cold inside sandwiches (tinned) or as a filling for baked potatoes; in curries, kedgerees, paellas, fish chowders, roulades, fisherman's pie, pasta bakes, pastries, mousses, kebabs or warm salads; baked, poached, grilled, fried (with or without batter), mashed with potatoes to make fishcakes, pickled or breadcrumbed; or eaten on their own, accompanied by rice or salad and bread.

Vegetable Delights

It is surprising how many ways vegetables can be used, when they are usually thought of as accompaniments to the meat-and-potatoes section of a meal. You can use vegetables in pasta dishes, curries, lasagnes, kebabs, pies, pastries, rice dishes, stir-fries, casseroles, stews, soups and salads. You can serve them roasted, baked (half an aubergine can be hollowed out, the flesh mixed with tomatoes and onion and the aubergine shell refilled with the mixture, then baked with cheese, for example), stuffed (peppers can be stuffed with rice or meat, for instance), barbecued, grilled within hot melts, made into vegetarian burgers and sausages or, of course, raw.

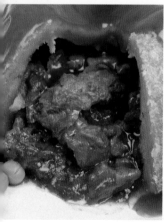

Cheap Cuts of Meat

People often think that meat is just too expensive to be part of the diet for someone living on a tight budget. But this is not actually the case. What is true is that people used to going to the supermarket to buy their meat will only be presented with the prices on the counter. More than that, they will only be offered meat from a limited selection of cuts and produce. This gives the false impression that meat is too expensive to be able to be part of a 'cheap meal challenge'.

Think Continental

One Hungarian gentleman of advanced years proclaimed 'I don't understand why young families these days say they cannot afford meat. We escaped from Hungary with nothing but the clothes on our backs and yet always ate well. But you Anglo-Saxons don't know about cheap cuts of meat.' Well, that is not entirely true. We do, or we did during the war years, but most of us have forgotten what these cuts are. Cheap cuts of meat include:

- Cheeks
- Trotters
- Liver
- Hock
- Shoulder
- Chump
- Oxtail
- Skirt
- Brisket
- Tongue (technically offal – *see* page 46)

Where Do You Get These?

These are all available at butchers and markets, particularly specialist meat markets. You can also buy some of them from the fresh meat sections of the larger superstores, although the variety will be restricted and you will be paying retail, not wholesale, prices.

How to Cook Cheap Cuts of Meat

The cheap cuts of meat are often less expensive because they tend to be tougher than the usual cuts such as T-bone or rib-eye. But they are also lean (less fatty) and, with the right treatment, are extremely tasty. Some suggestions include:

- **Cheeks** Beef cheeks are gaining in popularity in top restaurants, particularly as business people are reducing their entertainment budgets and exploring different options. Try slow-cooking beef cheeks in some red wine or a treacle and vinegar sauce for a few hours until tender. Serve hot in its juices with some creamy mash, roast parsnips and hot English mustard.

45

- Oxtail This is the tail of a steer or cow and is notoriously tough. Tenderise it and slow-cook it in a meaty broth until the juices permeate the liquid. Cut away the meat and boil it up in a stew, together with chunks of carrot, leeks and turnip or swede. Serve on its own or with baby new potatoes.

- Skirt This is the underpart, or belly, of a cow or lamb. This is a very lean meat and can take up to 6 hours until it is tender enough to eat. Tenderise it and put it in a slow-cooker or hay box along with some stock and chopped vegetables. When you get home, add some fresh dumplings and serve.

- Tongue Although technically offal, this is a delicious meat and can be bought very cheaply. It is also versatile, and can be used, when cold, as sandwich filling: add some ciabatta, onion relish and some salad leaves and provide yourself with a top-quality meat sandwich.

Offal

This is basically everything else left over when the main flesh has been taken from the carcass of an animal, such as head, brain, brawn, snout, tongue, tripe, giblets and so on. Dishes using offal were very popular even 40 years ago and were often sold as basic pub grub alongside the traditional steak and chips. However, there are various reasons why offal has lost its popularity, not least because of the meat scares of the 1990s, with CJD (the human variant of BSE) and scrapie, meaning that people shunned meat. Many are only just starting to come back to it but do not feel brave enough to deal with offal.

I Would Never Eat Those!

But you eat sausages, haggis and re-formed meat burgers – what do you think they use to make them? You might like to eat steak and kidney pie or liver as part of a mixed grill. You may have eaten Scrapple sandwiches in the States (using meat made from a combination of pig offal) and maybe munched through some Rocky Mountain Oysters, which are bulls' testes. Moreover, if you have eaten some of these things, you probably really enjoyed them.

A Last Word

There are so many ways to make a cheap meal that can include meat in various forms and fresh fish. You do not have to resort to bargain basement packets of burgers and fish fingers. When thinking about your own cheap meal challenge, try going beyond the boundaries of what you have been used to, or the 'easy' options presented by the supermarkets. The more you can cook these dishes, the more varied the menu will become, all the while sticking to your budget – and even cutting your budget further.

Case Study: The Appleyards

Christopher and Rhian Appleyard, from Surrey, and their student children Rachel (21) and Richard (19) tried the taste challenge. They found that they could plan and prepare a two-course meal well within £5 and still have some food – and change – left over. Rhian reports, 'This is a tried-and-tested regular meal: Turkey Spaghetti Bolognese with fresh tomatoes, and organic fruit yogurt for dessert. I usually keep a portion of the Bolognese for my lunch the next day so it serves five people, not four. I went to a well-known international supermarket chain to buy the ingredients.' The breakdown is:

- ∞ Turkey mince £1.78
- ∞ Own-brand mushroom pasta sauce 88p
- ∞ Own-brand basics range value spaghetti 39p
- ∞ Organic plum tomatoes 66p
- ∞ Biopot wholegrain peach yogurt £1.24

Total £4.95

Storing Food

❦

It sounds like common sense, but storing food is not something that many people today find easy, for various reasons. We tend to throw away what is left if we think it is 'too small a portion' or we cannot think where to put it. Sometimes we need to think about ways of storing it that will get the best out of that particular food. Then there is the question of cupboard space... Here are a few helpful pointers to make your food stretch further and keep safer.

The Big Freeze

Forget stuffing frozen pizzas, pies and ready meals into your freezer. In reality, you can freeze just about anything for a future date. Often, fridge-freezers or deep-freezer units will display on their doors the ideal length of time for various food groups to help you work out for how long food can be stored.

What Can You Freeze?

What can't you freeze? Did you know you can freeze:

- Milk
- Fruit
- Vegetables
- Soups
- Stews
- Leftovers
- Takeaways
- Bread (bagels, buns and fruit loaf too)

Special Offers

Buying 'big ticket' items such as meat or fish fillets on a two-for-one or special offer is a great idea. Make the most of this and buy twice as much (because you will save more in the long term). These are often in freezable containers already so storing them is easy (make sure you have room!).

Bake and Freeze

As we have seen, you can cook extra portions and freeze them ready for another meal, another day. This may seem like extra work, but cooking up all your 'old' vegetables, for example, into a stew and freezing it reduces food wastage and saves money. And some days, you just cannot find the time to cook; being able to simply open the freezer and find your meal ready-made is a blessing.

Keeping Your Freezer Clean

This may sound obvious but, when your freezer is chock-full of ice and frost, it can create problems, such as:

- A premium on space When the freezer is overly frosted, you cannot store as much as you would like to.

- Inefficient use of energy Because it is frosted up, the freezer has to work twice as hard to keep things cold. Therefore, it is using more energy. Because it is using more energy, it is ratcheting up your fuel bills.

- Blocked drainage Too much frost and ice can block up the freezer or fridge drainage, meaning leaks from the unit onto the floor.

- The hassle of defrosting Defrosting a freezer can take a long time and, if you chip away at the ice with a knife, this can damage the knife, the freezer or even you.

Storing Food

Tips for Efficiency

To keep your freezer or icebox at maximum efficiency, bear in mind the following:

- **Not too high** Keep it at a lower temperature setting – try turning it from 6 to 5, for example.

- **Regular turnover** Check regularly to see what food has been in the freezer for too long, and use it up.

- **A helping hand** Try using an anti-frost mat, which can be bought inexpensively over the internet or from most homeware stores.

Stocking Cupboards

There is a lot to be said for buying in bulk or getting family-size packs of food, but not if you let something fester in the back of your cupboard or your kitchen larder. That said, there are many food items which can be stored for a much longer time than you think outside of the fridge or freezer. This might help when you bulk buy or wonder what you are going to cook (see also pages 62–65 for key store cupboard ingredients).

Dried Food

We have explored the benefits of staple dried food such as pasta or rice, but here are a couple more pointers to help you live on a tight family budget without feeling the pain:

- **Longevity of dried food** It is worth stocking up on dried split peas, lentils, rice and other dried foodstuffs. They can keep for up to 18 months or more, meaning they can always be relied on for a rainy day. If you have bought in bulk, dried foods can last for a long time without you having to replace them.

- **Clean and dry means less waste** When a bag of rice has split, or the pasta box is nearly empty, do not just leave it in the cupboard; put the rest into a jar or small tin, label it well and put into the cupboard. This will help to keep it fresher for longer and reduce any accidental spillage.

Canned Food Pros

Tinned food also has longevity, but we are not advocating constructing a mini-Warhol of soup cans in your kitchen. However, canned food has several advantages:

- **Longevity equals bulk** Since it has such a long shelf life, tinned food can be bought in bulk without fear of wastage or the need to freeze.

- **Versatility** It can be used on its own, cold or as part of a cooked meal; soups can be used as sauces or thickeners for stews; and cans of beans, spaghetti hoops and similar items make quick, light and cheap meals.

- **Low cost** Most shops sell good-quality, low-cost versions of the big-name brands.

- **Convenience** Canned food is handy for days when you are ill or cannot get out to buy fresh ingredients.

Canned Food Cons

Watch out for:

- **Rust** Rusting on tins can be caused by steam and damp created by cooking, so cook with a window open or fan on where possible.

- **Dents** In tins with dents that have 'pierced' through to the contents, the food is probably off.

- **Bulges** Tins which are bulging should be steered clear of – the food is definitely off.

Out of Sight, But Not Out of Mind (Completely)

Long-life store cupboard ingredients can be put away into the cupboard and forgotten about until they are needed. But do make sure you check use-by dates, as it is easy to forget just how long some store-cupboard staples have been loitering on your shelves.

Storing Fruit and Vegetables

Many fruit and vegetables can be kept fresh, dried out, made up into preserves or sauces or even frozen whole. This makes it more than worthwhile to stock up when you see a great bargain on fresh produce or to start growing your own fresh fruit and vegetables! Here we look at storing fruit around the house or in the fridge.

Stoned Fruit

This is not casting aspersions on their smoking habits. 'Stoned fruit' refers to fruit that has a central kernel, or stone. These tend to be softer fruit, which are more easily bruised, and may require different approaches to storing compared with 'hard' fruit such as apples or pears. Although tomatoes do not have a stone, they are a soft fruit and can be stored in the same way as soft fruit can. Examples of stoned fruit are: apricots, avocados, cherries, lychees, nectarines, peaches and plums. Eat stoned fruit within a week, and bear the following in mind:

- **Choosing** Select unwrinkled, smooth-skinned fruits with no blemishes, free of soft spots or discolouration. This will ensure maximum life and quality.

- **Storing ripe fruit** Refrigerate ripe stoned fruit in a plastic bag and use within four days.

- **Ripening hard fruit** If the fruit is a little hard, leave it at room temperature for a few days to soften up, but check to make sure it is not getting overripe.

❧ **Just before eating** Any fruit whose skin you eat along with the flesh should be washed in running water to make sure you remove any harmful bacteria or dirt.

Hard Fruit

Hard fruit mainly describes apples, pears and pineapples. Different rules apply when storing each of these three fruit. It is not hard to store apples, as you can leave them for months on end before they go past the point of no return. This makes them an excellent budget food, as well as being versatile and able to be eaten fresh or cooked. The more ripe the apple, the longer it stores. Pears do not keep as long as apples – maybe a month or two maximum. Pineapples do not keep well at room temperature, and are best in the fridge. However, they can be frozen, juiced or pulped. Bear the following in mind if storing hard fruit outside of the fridge:

❧ **Ventilation** Hard fruit needs plenty of ventilation, so do not pack too closely together, and store in containers which are not airtight, such as a wooden bin or fruit crate. You can also store the fruit in plastic bags, as long as there is a hole in it to allow the air to circulate.

❧ **Temperature** If you can, keep the temperature between 3°C/37°F and 7°C/44°F. So, obviously, the main part of the house may not be the best place if you want the fruit to last a while – ideal places are attics, cellars, garden sheds or garages.

❧ **Light** Hard fruit stores longer if kept in the dark, another reason for storing the fruit in the locations suggested above.

❧ **'Bad influence'** Overripe or decaying fruit can have an adverse effect on surrounding fruit. Check the fruit for any 'bad' ones and throw them away.

❧ **Apples and pears** Apples keep well when individually wrapped in paper such as old newspaper or wrapped in straw. This protects them against contamination from any 'bad apples' as well. Pears need even more gentle handling, but do not like to be wrapped up.

Storing Food

Berries

This includes raspberries, blueberries, gooseberries, redcurrants, strawberries (which are not technically berries), blackcurrants, elderberries and blackberries. They all tend to go off within a few days at room temperature, and within a week in the fridge. However, they do freeze well, apart from strawberries (which might be best made up into a jam or preserve). Kiwi fruit should also be treated in the same way.

Citrus Fruit

This term includes lemons, limes, clementines, satsumas, oranges, grapefruit, mandarins, tangerines, kumquats and ugli fruit.

- ∾ **Fridge is best** Citrus fruit keeps better in the fridge than the fruit bowl.

- ∾ **A sliding scale** The most perishable citrus fruit is the loose-skinned tangerine, which keeps up to a week in the fridge. Other oranges can be refrigerated for two weeks or more. Lemons and limes can store for even longer in the fridge.

- ∾ **Wrapped but ventilated** Store them in a plastic bag, which has air ventilation, in the fridge.

Bananas

These are very difficult to store, as, if you put them in a fruit bowl, they will ripen the other fruit and cause them to go off. The same thing will happen if you put it in the fridge with other fruit (and tomatoes). Also, banana skins will go black in the fridge, while, if you chop them up, they will oxidise and turn brown, as will apples. Some tips for storing bananas are:

- ∾ **Segregation** Keep bananas away from other fruit by keeping them in a separate bowl or hanging them on a banana tree (which also protects them from bruising). Or keep them in a plastic bag for a few days at room temperature.

- ∾ **Protection** Store individual bananas in a 'banana case' to protect them from bruising when in your bag, for example. Check out www.bananaguard.com or www.bananabunker.com.

- ❧ **Preservation** Cover chopped bananas with a little lemon or orange juice before using them in pies or desserts.

- ❧ **Preparation** Freeze them whole when ripe, in a plastic bag. When they are defrosted they are perfect for cooking, as there is little need to blend them.

Storing Root Vegetables

Root vegetables (carrots, parsnips, turnips, swedes, potatoes), especially ones you have grown yourself, can be stored in a cool, covered place such as an attic, porch, garage, garden shed or cellar. They store well loosely laid out in wooden boxes or crates and, like apples, they like to be individually wrapped in paper or packed with straw, or you can layer them with newspaper and plenty of sand to keep them cool. Remove loose soil but do not wash the vegetables before storing, and clear out any rotten or bad vegetables.

Bulb Vegetables

Onions and garlic that you have grown yourself must be thoroughly dried out first, perhaps for two weeks in the sun, until the outer skins are dark and crackly, like paper. Trim the stems and store them in boxes or string bags, but keep them cool and in the shade.

Bins and Barrels

Some fruit and vegetables will keep for a long time in a cupboard or 'vegetable bin'. Onions, garlic, turnips and potatoes will keep well in a clean, dry wooden box in a cool cupboard and apples and hard pears (conference) will keep well in a clean, dry box or barrel.

Freezing Fruit and Vegetables

Freezing fruit is easy and can be done in many ways. Most fruits maintain a high level of quality for 8 to 12 months at freezing temperatures. Citrus fruit and juices keep for less – up to 6 months. Food may still be edible after these times, but may not taste as good. You can freeze fruit either as it is or in syrup.

❧   Storing Food

Freezing Fruit on Its Own

Unsweetened fruit will keep for a shorter amount of time than fruit with syrup. Here are some tips:

- **Preparation** Wash and prepare the fruit whole, halved or in quarters. If cutting into halves or quarters, discard any stones or cores.

- **Cooking** Apples, rhubarb, pears and plums freeze better if they are cooked first. Add a little brown sugar syrup to sharper apples and rhubarb, especially if they are cut up. This prevents oxidisation.

- **Bags of berries** Berries (except strawberries) should be frozen on a flat tray first for a few hours, then put into individual bags and labelled.

- **Whole fruit** Pack whole fruit into containers, leaving 2.5 cm/¹/₂ inch headspace as the fruit will expand when frozen. Seal, label and freeze.

Freezing Fruit in Syrup

The sugar in syrup will help preserve fruit even longer. Pack the cut fruit into containers as described above, then:

1. Cover with cold syrup solution (1 part sugar to 1 part water)
2. Add ½ teaspoon ascorbic acid per 1/1¾ pints syrup
3. Leave 2.5 cm/¹/₂ in headspace
4. Seal, label and freeze

Freezing Fruit for a Purée or Sauce

This is great for planning pie fillings or preserves. For fruit that is soft enough, press the raw fruit through a sieve (to remove pips) or blend it (if there are no pips). For firmer fruit, bring to the boil and then simmer it for 2 minutes in 250 ml/8 fl oz water to every 1.8 kg/4 lb of fruit, then press through a sieve or blend. Mix in ¹/₂ tablespoon lemon juice and 200 g/ 7 oz sugar (to taste, depending on tartness), to every

900 g/2 lb of purée. Pack into containers, leaving the same amount of headspace as before.

Freezing Juices

This is great for making into jams. When adding the sugar, use around 200 g/7 oz to each 1l/1³/₄ pints juice:

1. Press the fruit through a sieve
2. Simmer until soft in a saucepan with a shallow layer of water
3. Strain through a muslin or 'jam' cloth bag
4. Cool down the juice
5. Sweeten with sugar to taste
6. Pour into a container, leaving room for expansion
7. Freeze

Vegetables

You can freeze most vegetables in the same way as for fruit, only without adding the sugar. This is great for making vegetable purée for baby food, for example, or for storing leftover vegetables to be made up into a sauce or stew at a later date. You can even make carrot or beetroot juice to add to special blends and create a healthy drink. For fresh, uncooked vegetables you may need to blanch them before freezing – check out www.gardenguides.com/416-freezing-vegetables for advice on freezing vegetables.

Tupperware Makes a Comeback

It is now common knowledge that HM The Queen of England likes to put her cereals in Tupperware tubs. Although there is a known phobia of plastic containers, called 'Tupperware anxiety', it is fair to say that the majority of households will benefit from investing in sets of Tupperware or similar plastic tubs and containers.

Storing Food

What Can You Put in Them?

You can put anything into them, including:

- Soups
- Stews
- Fruit
- Lasagne
- Pasta dishes
- Rice
- Takeaways
- Vegetables
- Snacks
- Salads
- Curries
- Chocolate
- Ice cream
- Leftovers

Where Can You Put the Food Once It Is in the Tubs?

Anywhere! They can be put into the freezer, fridge or cupboard, depending on what you want to store. When you need it, you can put them into the microwave and they are also dishwasher friendly, although sometimes there can be slight discolouration depending on the type of dishwasher or detergent you use.

Other Benefits

Plastic containers are also useful for:

- **Transporting food** Sandwiches, or a lunch you have prepared, can be taken to school, work or on a picnic.

- **Protecting food** They can keep delicate food such as bananas or soft fruit safe from bruising.

- **Using as a stockpot** You can keep a plastic tub in the fridge, into which you can put various materials appropriate for stock (*see* page 40).

- **Keeping the air out** This way, cookies will not go soft and cakes will not go hard, for example.

- **Keeping smells in** Well-sealed containers will prevent 'smell contagion' from strong cheeses or garlicky food, for example.

- **Safety** Using well-sealed containers for different foodstuffs helps keep certain foods separate for family members with allergies, as well as raw meat separate from cooked meat or food.

Other Containers

This book is not about buying new tubs and pots to put your odds and ends of food in, but about helping you to save money. So look around at what you have in your house; you can make your budget go further if you use and reuse what you already have, rather than buying new.

Bags
If you do not have room in your icebox for pots and tubs, use heavy-duty, resealable freezer bags. Many of these can even be recycled, if you wash them out thoroughly and dry them before reusing.

Clips, Seals and Ties
Many freezer bags come with their own ties, but one often ends up using these for all sorts of food bags: open cereal packets, bags of potato chips or open bags of nuts, for example, all in an effort to keep food as fresh as possible without wastage.

- **Clips** You can buy tough food bag clips to help keep dry food dry and prevent it from spilling out into the box or the cupboard. These can be washed and used again.

Storing Food

- **Clothes pegs** Rather than buying special food ties or clips, you can use old wooden or plastic clothes pegs. Remember to wash and dry them first!

- **Old hair clips** Children's discarded hair clips are great for using on dry food packets.

- **Elastic bands** You may need different sizes, depending on how big the packet is, but rubber bands can be very versatile.

- **Sticky tape** This is great but is not reusable and often loses its stickiness before the packet is finished (the same goes for the resealable tabs that often come with packaging).

Reusing Containers
Rather than buy new tubs or pots, you can always make the most of the following:

- **Takeaway containers** The plastic boxes from the Chinese takeout you had in a moment of weakness can be used in the same way as bought plastic boxes – in the fridge, freezer and microwave, and as lunchboxes.

- **Ready-roast tins** If you buy frozen joints, they sometimes come in their own foil container. Shop-bought pies also have foil dishes that can be used to store or to cook in, if treated carefully – do not put foil in the microwave!

- **Tins and cans** Keep those old coffee or biscuit tins: small, cylindrical tins can be used to store the remnants of dried food such as rice or sugar; tall, cylindrical tins can be used to store dried spaghetti; large, round tins make excellent cake tins; and square tins can be used to store open flour or keep bread rolls fresh.

Labelling is Critical

Whether you are freezing or storing food for a shorter period of time, it is vital that you label things clearly, especially if you have put one foodstuff into another's container. As well as reminding you of the contents of a container, it also enables you to check the date you froze or stored the food in order to know whether it should still be edible or not. Even if you can remember what you have put in a certain container, clear labelling enables other members of the family to know what it is, what ingredients are in it and to identify food that may be unsuitable for those with special dietary needs. Clear labelling also facilitates quick identification when in a hurry.

Keeping Things out of Reach

One of the best ways to keep costs down often involves willpower! Snacking is fine every now and then, but often people tend to 'graze' on whatever they find around. If you have teenagers, you will know they have a predisposition towards eating everything that is in the house, despite having eaten three hearty meals during the day.

Lock the Cupboard

You may already lock the alcohol cupboard, but why not put more expensive snacks such as chocolates in a locked cupboard? Treats are not prohibited from the food budget, but they can go very quickly so, by keeping hold of the key, they remain as treats, not as something to be munched throughout the day.

Out of Sight, Out of Reach

For smaller children, putting snacks and tasty treats into a particular tub and in a top cupboard may be a good way to stop little fingers getting to them. However, please make sure that your child does not get to know where they are – climbing accidents do happen frequently in the home. Try moving the snack box around to different locations every now and then.

Doing It by Halves

One pensioner tricks her twenty-something boys by taking half of her savoury snacks out of the box and hiding them in another container. This means they cannot eat everything.

Storing Food

Key Store-Cupboard Ingredients

It is essential to have a store cupboard full of ingredients that form the basis of many meals, or that you particularly like to use. Many store cupboard ingredients tend to have long shelf lives and to be used in fairly small quantities, so you only need to spend on them now and then. Obviously you can add to them at any time. One word of caution, however: do not buy very large bottles, packets or tubs until you know how much you will use them.

What to Buy for the Recipes in this Book

Below is a comprehensive list of 'store cupboard ingredients' that are featured in the recipes in this book – remember, these should only add to the cost of a meal occasionally, as you should not have to buy them each time you make a specific dish.

  Oil For cooking, use olive, sunflower, vegetable or groundnut oil. Do not cook with extra virgin olive oil – reserve that for things such as salad dressings. Cooking destroys the delicate flavour and aroma of extra virgin olive oil and, as it is the most expensive oil, it is simply a waste to cook with it.

  Vinegars When vinegar is called for, white wine vinegar is often a good option, as it will impart a more delicate flavour than a vinegar such as malt or cider, and it is not as expensive as balsamic or rice wine vinegar. It is a very versatile vinegar and can be used in stews and casseroles as well as sauces and marinades and Asian-style dishes such as stir-fries.

Stock cubes or powders Chicken, beef, vegetable and perhaps fish stock cubes are essential (unless you've made your own stock!).

Spices These are especially useful if spicy food is a firm favourite. Remember to keep them in a cool, dark place so as to preserve their pungency and aroma. Useful dried spices are: ground cumin, ground coriander, ground cinnamon, turmeric, paprika, ground ginger, chilli powder, cayenne pepper, salt, black pepper, mixed spices, ground ginger, Chinese five-spice powder and curry powder. You can also buy many of these unground, as seeds, which you grind yourself with a pestle and mortar, for even more flavour. Curry paste, in Korma or Madras varieties, for example, also goes a fairly long way. Even saffron is not necessarily out of your league, as, despite being the most expensive spice, you need very little to add a special flavour and colour to dishes. And, properly stored, saffron strands can last for several years. If you prefer, turmeric can always be used in place of saffron in order to impart colour.

Herbs Dried herbs are much cheaper than fresh (but if you grow your own herbs then great!). Again, store in a cool, dark place and buy in small quantities. Good ones to have are oregano, thyme, sage, parsley and mixed herbs.

Plain and self-raising flour These are essential store cupboard ingredients. Plain flour is used for making pastry (so much cheaper than buying it), biscuits and cookies, thickening casseroles and stews, savoury sauces and gravies and coating food prior to shallow frying. Self-raising flour ensures perfect cakes and baked puddings, as the ratio of raising agent and flour has already been measured out. This means there is less need to buy separate baking powder or bicarbonate of soda.

Cornflour This is used to thicken sauces – especially useful if watching calorie intake.

Tomato purée This is best if bought in a tube, then, once opened, stored in the refrigerator to give it the best shelf life.

Soy and hoisin sauce Either dark or light soy sauce. Dark soy sauce tends to be slightly thicker, sweeter and richer. Hoisin sauce is a ready-made dipping sauce, which includes soy sauce in its ingredients, but it is also used as a cooking ingredient.

Other sauces There are so many to choose from, so only buy them if you think you are going to get a good deal of use out of them. Hot pepper sauce, Tabasco or sweet chilli sauce are some that might be valuable.

Clear honey Buy in a squeezy bottle as this makes it easier to use.

Sugar This is useful for many recipes, and having a selection is worthwhile, especially if you bake. Ideal sugars to stock would be granulated, caster, soft brown and icing sugar.

Store-Cupboard Items You Will Need To Buy More Often

Canned tomatoes Probably one of the most frequently used canned items. Whole tomatoes in cans are cheaper to buy than the chopped variety.

Canned beans and pulses Mixed beans, kidney beans, cannellini beans and chickpeas are commonly used pulses.

Pasta You'll get through a lot of this but it is cheap and stores well. Two good staples to have are penne and spaghetti.

- ❧ Rice Similar staple to pasta. Main types to have are long-grain or basmati, both white and brown, and risotto rice.

- ❧ Other grains Couscous and lentils are also versatile and handy to have to hand.

Store-Cupboard Nonessentials

What you buy partially depends on your situation in life – for instance, there are many items that may be appropriate (or more realistic) for a student's store cupboard, but which are a false economy for a family's budget and health, or should be made rather than bought:

- ❧ Tinned pulses and beans It is better to buy these dry and in bulk, as they are cheaper and last longer – although it involves forethought, as they may need long soaking.

- ❧ Microwave rice It is better to buy bulk dry rice and cook your own.

- ❧ Pasta-bake sauces Not for a group or a family – it is far cheaper to make your own.

- ❧ Tinned fruit and vegetables This can be useful for trifles and pies, but steer clear of tinned vegetables except perhaps sweetcorn or butter beans.

- ❧ Tinned meat pies Big no-no for the family – cook your own out of leftovers to save several the pennies. Same goes for tinned meat curry.

- ❧ Tinned red salmon Pink salmon is cheaper in tins, while mackerel and sardines are even cheaper.

Soups and

Starters

This section will show you how to add a little extra to your meal without spending a fortune, or make a soup filling enough for a main course – ever the budget star. The Rich Tomato Soup with Roasted Red Peppers or the Classic Minestrone will be perfect to warm you up on a cold day, while the Bruschetta with Pecorino, Garlic & Tomatoes is an excellent crunchy delight to start you off.

Rich Tomato Soup with Roasted Red Peppers

Serves 4

2 tbsp olive oil

4 red peppers, halved and deseeded

450 g/1 lb ripe plum tomatoes, halved

2 onions, unpeeled and quartered

4 garlic cloves, unpeeled

600 ml/1 pint chicken or vegetable stock

salt and freshly ground black pepper

4 tbsp sour cream

1 tbsp freshly shredded basil

Preheat the oven to 200°C/400°F/Gas Mark 6, 15 minutes before roasting. Lightly oil a roasting tin with 1 teaspoon of the olive oil.

Place the peppers and tomatoes cut-side down in the roasting tin with the onion quarters and the garlic cloves. Spoon over the remaining oil. Bake in the preheated oven for 30 minutes, or until the skins on the peppers have started to blacken and blister.

Allow the vegetables to cool for about 10 minutes, then remove the skins, stalks and seeds from the peppers. Peel away the skins from the tomatoes and onions and squeeze out the garlic.

Place the cooked vegetables into a blender or food processor and blend until smooth. Add the stock and blend again to form a smooth purée.

If a smooth soup is preferred, strain the puréed soup through a sieve. Pour into a saucepan. Bring to the boil, simmer gently for 2–3 minutes, and season to taste with salt and pepper. Serve hot with a swirl of sour cream and a sprinkling of shredded basil on the top.

Italian Bean Soup

Serves 4

2 tsp olive oil
1 leek, washed and chopped
1 garlic clove, peeled and crushed
2 tsp dried oregano
75 g/3 oz green beans, trimmed
and cut into bite-size pieces
410 g can cannellini beans,
drained and rinsed
75 g/3 oz small pasta shapes
1 litre/1³/₄ pint vegetable stock
8 cherry tomatoes
salt and freshly ground
black pepper
3 tbsp freshly shredded
basil (optional)

Heat the oil in a large saucepan. Add the leek, garlic and oregano and cook gently for 5 minutes, stirring occasionally.

Stir in the green beans and the cannellini beans. Sprinkle in the pasta and pour in the stock.

Bring the stock mixture to the boil, then reduce the heat to a simmer.

Cook for 12–15 minutes until the vegetables are tender and the pasta is cooked to al dente. Stir occasionally.

In a heavy-based frying pan, dry-fry the tomatoes over a high heat until they soften and the skins begin to blacken.

Gently crush the tomatoes in the pan with the back of a spoon and add to the soup.

Season to taste with salt and pepper. Stir in the shredded basil, if using, and serve immediately.

Cream of Pumpkin Soup

Serves 4

700 g/1 1/2 lb pumpkin flesh (after peeling and discarding the seeds)
2 tbsp olive oil
1 onion, peeled
1 leek, trimmed
1 carrot, peeled
2 celery stalks
4 garlic cloves, peeled and crushed
1.7 litres/3 pints water
salt and freshly ground black pepper
1/4 tsp freshly grated nutmeg
150 ml/1/4 pint single cream
1/4 tsp cayenne pepper
warm herby bread, to serve

Cut the skinned and deseeded pumpkin flesh into 2.5 cm/1 inch cubes. Heat the olive oil in a large saucepan and cook the pumpkin for 2–3 minutes, coating it completely with oil. Chop the onion and leek finely and cut the carrot and celery into small dice.

Add the vegetables to the saucepan with the garlic and cook, stirring, for 5 minutes, or until they have begun to soften. Cover the vegetables with the water and bring to the boil. Season with plenty of salt and pepper and the nutmeg, cover and simmer for 15–20 minutes until all of the vegetables are tender.

When the vegetables are tender, remove from the heat, cool slightly, then pour into a food processor or blender. Liquidise to form a smooth purée, then pass through a sieve into a clean saucepan.

Adjust the seasoning to taste and add all but 2 tablespoons of the cream and enough water to obtain the correct consistency. Bring the soup to the boil, add the cayenne pepper and serve immediately, swirled with the remaining cream and the warm herby bread.

Bacon ❧ Split Pea Soup

Serves 4

50 g/2 oz dried split peas
25 g/1 oz margarine or butter
1 garlic clove, peeled and
finely chopped
1 medium onion, peeled and
thinly sliced
125 g/4 oz long-grain rice
2 tbsp tomato purée
1.1 litres/2 pints vegetable or
chicken stock
175 g/ 6 oz carrots, peeled and
finely diced
125 g/4 oz streaky bacon,
finely chopped
salt and freshly ground
black pepper
2 tbsp freshly chopped parsley
4 tbsp single cream
warm, crusty garlic bread,
to serve

Cover the dried split peas with plenty of cold water, cover loosely and leave to soak for a minimum of 12 hours, or preferably overnight.

Melt the margarine or butter in a heavy-based saucepan, add the garlic and onion and cook for 2–3 minutes, without colouring. Add the rice, drained split peas and tomato purée and cook for 2–3 minutes, stirring constantly to prevent sticking. Add the stock, bring to the boil, then reduce the heat and simmer for 20–25 minutes until the rice and peas are tender. Remove from the heat and leave to cool.

Blend about three quarters of the soup in a food processor or blender to form a smooth purée. Pour the purée into the remaining soup in the saucepan. Add the carrots to the saucepan and cook for a further 10–12 minutes until the carrots are tender.

Meanwhile, place the bacon in a nonstick frying pan and cook over a gentle heat until the bacon is crisp. Remove and drain on absorbent kitchen paper.

Season the soup with salt and pepper to taste, then stir in the parsley and cream. Reheat for 2–3 minutes, then ladle into soup bowls. Sprinkle with the bacon and serve immediately with warm garlic bread.

Classic Minestrone

Serves 4–6

25 g/1 oz margarine or butter
1 tbsp olive oil
2 rashers streaky bacon
1 onion, peeled
1 garlic clove, peeled
1 celery stalk, trimmed
2 carrots, peeled
400 g can whole peeled
tomatoes, chopped
1.1 litre/2 pints vegetable or
chicken stock
125 g/4 oz green cabbage,
finely shredded
50 g/2 oz French beans, trimmed
and halved
3 tbsp frozen petits pois
50 g/2 oz spaghetti, broken into
short pieces
salt and freshly ground
black pepper
Parmesan cheese shavings,
to garnish
crusty bread, to serve

Heat the margarine or butter and olive oil together in a large saucepan. Chop the bacon and add to the saucepan. Cook for 3–4 minutes, then remove with a slotted spoon and reserve.

Finely chop the onion, garlic, celery and carrots and add to the saucepan, one ingredient at a time, stirring well after each addition. Cover and cook gently for 8–10 minutes until the vegetables are softened.

Add the chopped tomatoes, with their juice and the stock, bring to the boil, then cover the saucepan with a lid, reduce the heat and simmer gently for about 20 minutes.

Stir in the cabbage, beans, peas and spaghetti pieces. Cover and simmer for a further 20 minutes, or until all the ingredients are tender. Season to taste with salt and pepper.

Return the cooked bacon to the saucepan and bring the soup to the boil. Serve the soup immediately with Parmesan cheese shavings sprinkled on the top and plenty of crusty bread to accompany it.

Pumpkin ❧ Smoked Haddock Soup

Serves 4

2 tbsp olive or sunflower oil
1 medium onion,
peeled and chopped
2 garlic cloves, peeled and chopped
1 celery stalk, trimmed and chopped
450 g/1 lb pumpkin,
peeled, deseeded and
cut into chunks
450 g/1 lb potatoes, peeled and
cut into chunks
900 ml/1 1/2 pints fish or chicken
stock, heated
175 g/6 oz smoked haddock fillet
150 ml/1/4 pint milk
freshly ground black pepper
2 tbsp freshly chopped parsley

Heat the oil in a large, heavy-based saucepan and gently cook the onion, garlic and celery for about 10 minutes. This will release the sweetness but not colour the vegetables. Add the pumpkin and potatoes to the saucepan and stir to coat the vegetables with the oil.

Gradually pour in the stock and bring to the boil. Cover, then reduce the heat and simmer for 25 minutes, stirring occasionally. Remove the saucepan from the heat and leave to cool for 5–10 minutes.

Blend the mixture in a food processor or blender to form a chunky purée and return to the cleaned saucepan.

Meanwhile, place the fish in a shallow frying pan. Pour in the milk with 3 tablespoons water and bring almost to boiling point. Reduce the heat, cover and simmer for 6 minutes, or until the fish is cooked and flakes easily. Remove from the heat and, using a slotted spoon, remove the fish from the liquid, reserving both liquid and fish.

Discard the skin and any bones from the fish and flake into pieces. Stir the fish liquid into the soup, together with the flaked fish. Season with freshly ground black pepper, stir in the parsley and serve immediately.

Smoked Mackerel Vol-au-Vents

Serves 4

350 g/12 oz ready-made puff pastry
flour, for dusting
1 small egg, beaten
2 tsp sesame seeds
225 g/8 oz peppered smoked
mackerel, skinned and chopped
5 cm/2 inch piece cucumber
4 tbsp soft cream cheese
2 tbsp cranberry sauce
1 tbsp freshly chopped dill
1 tbsp finely grated lemon zest
dill sprigs, to garnish
mixed salad leaves,
to serve

Preheat the oven to 230°C/450°F/Gas Mark 8, 15 minutes before baking. Roll the pastry out on a lightly floured surface and, using a 9 cm/3½ inch fluted cutter, cut out eight rounds.

Using a 1 cm/¹/₂ inch cutter, mark a lid in the centre of four of the rounds. Place the plain rounds on a damp baking sheet and brush them with a little beaten egg. Place the remaining rounds (with marked lids) on top and press the edges lightly together.

Sprinkle the pastry with the sesame seeds and bake in the preheated oven for 10–12 minutes until golden brown and well risen.

Transfer the vol-au-vents to a chopping board and, when cool enough to touch, carefully remove the lids with a small, sharp knife. Scoop out any uncooked pastry from the inside of each vol-au-vent, then return to the oven for 5–8 minutes to dry out. Remove and allow to cool.

Flake the mackerel into small pieces and reserve. Peel the cucumber if desired, cut into very small dice and add to the mackerel.

Beat the soft cream cheese with the cranberry sauce, chopped dill and lemon zest. Stir in the mackerel and cucumber and use to fill the vol-au-vents. Place the lids on top, garnish with dill sprigs and serve with mixed salad leaves.

Mozzarella Frittata with Tomato & Basil Salad

Serves 4

For the salad:

4 ripe but firm tomatoes
1 tbsp fresh basil leaves
2 tbsp olive oil
1 tbsp fresh lemon juice
1 tsp caster sugar
freshly ground black pepper

For the frittata:

5 medium eggs, beaten
pinch salt
200 g/7 oz mozzarella cheese
2 spring onions, trimmed and finely chopped
1 tbsp olive oil
warm crusty bread, to serve

To make the tomato and basil salad, slice the tomatoes very thinly, tear up the basil leaves and sprinkle over. Make the dressing by whisking the olive oil, lemon juice and sugar together well. Season with black pepper before drizzling the dressing over the salad.

To make the frittata, preheat the grill to a high heat just before beginning to cook. Place the eggs in a large bowl with the salt and whisk. Grate the mozzarella and stir into the egg with the finely chopped spring onions.

Heat the oil in a large, nonstick frying pan and pour in the egg mixture, stirring with a wooden spoon to spread the ingredients evenly over the pan.

Cook on the hob for 5–8 minutes until the frittata is golden brown and firm on the underside. Place the whole pan under the preheated grill and cook for about 4–5 minutes until the top is golden brown. Slide the frittata onto a serving plate, cut into four large wedges and serve immediately with the tomato and basil salad and plenty of warm crusty bread.

Sweetcorn Fritters

Serves 4

4 tbsp groundnut oil
1 small onion, peeled and finely chopped
1 red chilli, deseeded and finely chopped
1 garlic clove, peeled and crushed
1 tsp ground coriander
325 g can sweetcorn
6 spring onions, trimmed and finely sliced
1 medium egg, lightly beaten
salt and freshly ground black pepper
3 tbsp plain flour
1 tsp baking powder
spring onion curls, to garnish
Thai-style chutney, to serve

Heat 1 tablespoon of the groundnut oil in a frying pan, add the onion and cook gently for 7–8 minutes until beginning to soften. Add the chilli, garlic and ground coriander and cook for 1 minute, stirring continuously. Remove from the heat.

Drain the sweetcorn and tip into a mixing bowl. Lightly mash with a potato masher to break down the corn a little. Add the cooked onion mixture to the bowl with the spring onions and beaten egg. Season to taste with salt and pepper, then stir to mix together. Sift the flour and baking powder over the mixture and stir in.

Heat 2 tablespoons of the groundnut oil in a large frying pan. Drop 4 or 5 heaped teaspoonfuls of the sweetcorn mixture into the pan and, using a fish slice or spatula, flatten each to make a 1 cm/$1/2$ inch-thick fritter.

Fry the fritters for 3 minutes, or until golden brown on the underside, turn over and fry for a further 3 minutes, or until cooked through and crisp.

Remove the fritters from the pan and drain on absorbent kitchen paper. Keep warm while cooking the remaining fritters, adding a little more oil if needed. Garnish with spring onion curls and serve immediately with a Thai-style chutney.

Peperonata
(Braised Mixed Peppers)

Serves 4

1 green pepper
1 red pepper
1 yellow pepper
1 orange pepper
1 onion, peeled
2 garlic cloves, peeled
4 very ripe tomatoes
2 tbsp olive oil
1 tbsp freshly chopped oregano
salt and freshly ground
black pepper
150 ml/¹/₄ pint chicken or
vegetable stock
fresh oregano sprigs,
to garnish
focaccia or flatbread,
to serve

Remove the seeds from the peppers and cut into thin strips. Slice the onion into rings and chop the garlic cloves finely.

Make a cross on the top of each tomato, then place in a bowl and cover with boiling water. Allow to stand for about 2 minutes. Drain, then remove the skins and seeds and chop the tomato flesh into cubes.

Heat the olive oil in a frying pan and fry the peppers, onion and garlic for 5–10 minutes until soft and lightly coloured. Stir continuously.

Add the tomatoes and oregano to the peppers and onion and season to taste with salt and pepper. Cover the pan and bring to the boil. Simmer gently for about 30 minutes until tender, adding the chicken or vegetable stock halfway through the cooking time.

Garnish with sprigs of oregano and serve hot with plenty of freshly baked focaccia bread. Alternatively, lightly toast slices of flatbread and pile a spoonful of peperonata onto each plate.

Pasta with Walnut Sauce

Serves 4

40 g/1¹/₂ oz shelled
walnuts, toasted
3 spring onions, trimmed
and chopped
2 garlic cloves, peeled
and sliced
1 tbsp freshly chopped parsley
or basil
3 tbsp olive oil
salt and freshly ground
black pepper
225 g/8 oz broccoli,
cut into florets
175 g/6 oz pasta shapes
1 red chilli, deseeded and finely
chopped

Place the toasted walnuts in a blender or food processor with the chopped spring onions, one of the garlic cloves and the parsley or basil. Blend to a fairly smooth paste, then gradually add 1–2 tablespoons of the olive oil until it is well mixed into the paste. Season the walnut paste to taste with salt and pepper and reserve.

Bring a large pan of lightly salted water to a rolling boil. Add the broccoli, return to the boil and cook for 2 minutes. Remove the broccoli using a slotted draining spoon and refresh under cold running water. Drain again and pat dry on absorbent kitchen paper.

Bring the water back to a rolling boil. Add the pasta and cook according to the packet instructions, or until *al dente*.

Meanwhile, heat the remaining oil in a frying pan. Add the remaining garlic and the chilli. Cook gently for 2 minutes, or until softened. Add the broccoli and walnut paste. Cook for a further 3–4 minutes until heated through.

Drain the pasta thoroughly and transfer to a large, warmed serving bowl. Pour over the walnut and broccoli sauce. Toss together, adjust the seasoning and serve immediately.

Olive & Feta Parcels

Makes 6

1 small red pepper
1 small yellow pepper
125 g/4 oz assorted marinated
green and black olives
125 g/4 oz feta cheese
2 tbsp pine nuts, lightly toasted
6 sheets filo pastry
3 tbsp olive oil
sour cream and chive dip,
to serve

Preheat the oven to 180°C/350°F/Gas Mark 4, 10 minutes before baking. Preheat the grill, then line the grill rack with foil.

Cut the peppers into quarters and remove the seeds. Place skin-side up on the foil-lined grill rack and cook under the preheated grill for 10 minutes, turning occasionally, until the skins begin to blacken. Place the peppers in a polythene bag and leave until cool enough to handle, then skin and thinly slice.

Chop the olives and cut the feta cheese into small cubes. Mix together the olives, feta, sliced peppers and pine nuts.

Cut one sheet of filo pastry in half, then brush one half with a little of the oil. Place a spoonful of the olive and feta mix one third of the way up the pastry half. Fold over the pastry and wrap to form a square parcel encasing the filling completely.

Place this parcel in the centre of the second half of the pastry sheet. Brush the edges lightly with a little oil, bring up the corners to meet in the centre and twist them loosely to form a purse. Brush with a little more oil and repeat with the remaining filo pastry and filling.

Place the parcels on a lightly oiled baking sheet and bake in the preheated oven for 10–15 minutes until crisp and golden brown. Serve with the dip.

Bruschetta with Pecorino, Garlic & Tomatoes

Serves 4

6 ripe but firm tomatoes
125 g/4 oz pecorino cheese,
finely grated
1 tbsp oregano leaves
salt and freshly ground
black pepper
3 tbsp olive oil
3 garlic cloves, peeled
8 slices flat Italian bread,
such as focaccia
50 g/2 oz mozzarella cheese, sliced
marinated black olives,
to serve

Preheat the grill and line the grill rack with foil just before cooking. Make a small cross in the top of each tomato, then place in a small bowl and cover with boiling water. Leave to stand for 2 minutes, then drain and remove the skins. Cut into quarters, remove the seeds and chop the flesh into small dice.

Mix the tomato flesh with the pecorino cheese and 2 teaspoons of the fresh oregano and season to taste with salt and pepper. Add 1 tablespoon of the olive oil and mix thoroughly.

Crush the garlic and spread evenly over the bread slices. Heat 2 tablespoons of the olive oil in a large frying pan and fry the bread slices until they are crisp and golden.

Place the fried bread on a lightly oiled baking tray and spoon on the tomato and cheese topping. Place a little mozzarella on top and place under the preheated grill for 3–4 minutes until golden and bubbling. Garnish with the remaining oregano, then arrange the bruschettas on a serving plate and serve immediately with the olives.

Mozzarella Parcels with Cranberry Relish

Serves 4

75 g/3 oz mozzarella cheese
8 slices thin white bread
2 medium eggs, beaten
salt and freshly ground
black pepper
oil for deep frying, preferably olive oil

For the cranberry relish:

125 g/4 oz cranberries,
thawed if frozen
2 tbsp fresh orange juice
grated zest of 1 small orange
50 g/2 oz soft light brown sugar
1 tbsp port, or use extra orange juice

Slice the mozzarella thinly, remove the crusts from the bread and make sandwiches with the bread and cheese. Cut into 5 cm/2 inch squares and squash them quite flat. Season the eggs with salt and pepper, then soak the bread in the seasoned egg for 1 minute on each side until well coated.

Heat the oil to 190°C/375°F and deep-fry the bread squares for 1–2 minutes until they are crisp and golden brown. Drain on absorbent kitchen paper and keep warm while the cranberry relish is prepared.

Place the cranberries, orange juice, zest, sugar and port, if using, into a small saucepan and add 5 tablespoons water. Bring to the boil, then simmer for 10 minutes, or until the cranberries have 'popped'. Sweeten with a little more sugar if necessary.

Arrange the mozzarella parcels on individual serving plates. Serve with a little of the cranberry relish.

Fish & Seafood

Fish and seafood is not only an economical meal option, but a tasty and healthy one as well! Why not try something different and have Fish Crumble or Tuna Fish Burgers for dinner tonight, or try something deliciously Mediterranean like the Spanish Omelette with Smoked Cod or the Marinated Mackerel with Tomato & Basil Salad?

Spanish Omelette
with Smoked Cod

Serves 3–4

125 g/4 oz smoked cod
3 tbsp sunflower oil
350 g/12 oz potatoes, peeled and
cut into 1 cm/¹/₂ inch cubes
2 onions, peeled and cut into wedges
2–4 large garlic cloves, peeled
and thinly sliced
1 large red pepper, deseeded,
quartered and thinly sliced
25 g/1 oz margarine or
butter, melted
6 eggs, beaten
salt and freshly ground
black pepper
2 tbsp freshly chopped
flat-leaf parsley
50 g/2 oz mature Cheddar
cheese, grated

To serve:

crusty bread
tossed green salad

Place the cod in a shallow dish and pour over boiling water. Leave for 5 minutes, then drain and allow to cool. When cool, discard the skin and any pin bones and cut into small pieces.

Heat the oil in a large, nonstick, heavy-based frying pan, add the potatoes, onions and garlic and cook gently for 10–15 minutes until golden brown, then add the red pepper. Place the cod on top of the vegetables and cook for 3 minutes.

When the vegetables are cooked, drain off any excess oil. Beat the margarine or butter into the eggs, season, then stir in the parsley. Pour the egg mixture over the top of the vegetables and cod and cook gently for 5 minutes, or until the eggs become firm.

Sprinkle the grated cheese over the top and place the pan under a preheated hot grill. Cook for 2–3 minutes until the cheese is golden and bubbling. Carefully slide the omelette onto a large plate and serve immediately with plenty of bread and salad.

Smoked Haddock Tart

Serves 6

For the shortcrust pastry:

150 g/5 oz plain flour
pinch salt
25 g/1 oz white vegetable fat,
cut into small cubes
40 g/1¹/₂ oz butter or hard margarine,
cut into small cubes

For the filling:

225 g/8 oz smoked haddock,
skinned and cubed
2 large eggs, beaten
300 ml/¹/₂ pint single cream
1 tsp Dijon mustard
freshly ground black pepper
125 g/4 oz Gruyère cheese, grated
1 tbsp freshly snipped chives

To serve:

lemon wedges
tomato wedges
fresh green salad leaves

Preheat the oven to 190°C/375°F/Gas Mark 5, 10 minutes before baking. To make the pastry, sift the flour and salt into a large bowl. Add the fats and mix lightly. Using the fingertips, rub into the flour until the mixture resembles breadcrumbs. Sprinkle 1 tablespoon cold water into the mixture and, with a knife, start bringing the dough together. (It may be necessary to use the hands for the final stage.) If the dough does not form a ball instantly, add a little more water. Put the pastry in a polythene bag and chill for at least 30 minutes.

On a lightly floured surface, roll out the pastry and use to line an 18 cm/7 inch, lightly oiled quiche or flan tin. Prick the base all over with a fork and bake blind in the preheated oven for 15 minutes.

Carefully remove the pastry from the oven and brush with a little of the beaten egg. Return to the oven for a further 5 minutes, then place the fish in the pastry case.

For the filling, beat together the eggs and cream. Add the mustard, black pepper and cheese and pour over the fish. Sprinkle with the chives and bake for 35–40 minutes until the filling is golden brown and set in the centre. Serve hot or cold with the lemon and tomato wedges and salad leaves.

Fish Puff Tart

Serves 4

350 g/12 oz ready-made puff
pastry, thawed if frozen
plain flour, for dusting
150 g/5 oz smoked haddock
150 g/5 oz pollack or whiting
1 tbsp pesto
2 tomatoes, sliced
125 g/4 oz goats' cheese, sliced
1 medium egg, beaten
freshly chopped parsley,
to garnish

Preheat the oven to 220°C/425°F/Gas Mark 7. On a lightly floured surface, roll out the pastry into a 20 x 25 cm/8 x 10 inch rectangle.

Draw an 18 x 23 cm/7 x 9 inch rectangle in the centre of the pastry to form a 2.5 cm/1 inch border. (Take care not to cut through the pastry.)

Lightly cut crisscross patterns in the border of the pastry with a knife.

Place the fish on a chopping board and skin with a sharp knife. Cut into thin slices.

Spread the pesto evenly over the bottom of the pastry case with the back of a spoon.

Arrange the fish, tomatoes and cheese in the pastry case and brush the pastry with the beaten egg.

Bake the tart in the preheated oven for 20–25 minutes until the pastry is well risen, puffed and golden brown. Garnish with the chopped parsley and serve immediately.

Marinated Mackerel with Tomato & Basil Salad

Serves 4

4 mackerel, filleted
4 beefsteak tomatoes, sliced
75 g/3 oz watercress
2 oranges, peeled and segmented
75 g/3 oz mozzarella cheese, sliced
2 tbsp basil leaves, shredded
fresh basil sprig, to garnish

For the marinade:

juice of 1 lemon
3 tbsp olive oil
2 tbsp basil leaves

For the dressing:

1 tbsp lemon juice
1 tsp Dijon mustard
1 tsp caster sugar
salt and freshly ground
black pepper
3 tbsp olive oil

Remove as many of the fine pin bones as possible from the mackerel fillets, lightly rinse and pat dry with absorbent kitchen paper and place in a shallow dish.

Blend the marinade ingredients together and pour over the mackerel fillets. Make sure the marinade has covered the fish completely. Cover and leave in a cool place for at least 8 hours, but preferably overnight. As the fillets marinate, they will lose their translucency and look as if they are cooked.

Place the tomatoes, watercress, oranges and mozzarella cheese in a large bowl and toss. To make the dressing, whisk the lemon juice with the mustard, sugar, seasoning and oil in a bowl. Pour over half the dressing, toss again and then arrange on a serving platter.

Remove the mackerel from the marinade, cut into bite-size pieces and sprinkle with the shredded basil. Arrange on top of the salad, drizzle over the remaining dressing, scatter with basil leaves and garnish with a basil sprig. Serve.

Smoked Haddock Kedgeree

Serves 4

300 g/10 oz smoked haddock fillets
50 g/2 oz margarine or butter
1 onion, peeled and finely chopped
2 tsp mild curry powder
175 g/6 oz long-grain rice
450 ml/³/₄ pint fish or vegetable
stock, heated
2 large eggs, hard-boiled
and shelled
2 tbsp freshly chopped parsley
salt and freshly ground
black pepper
pinch cayenne pepper

Place the haddock in a shallow frying pan and cover with 300 ml/¹/₂ pint water. Simmer gently for 8–10 minutes until the fish is cooked.

Drain, then remove all the skin and bones from the fish and flake into a dish. Keep warm.

Melt the margarine or butter in a saucepan and add the chopped onion and curry powder. Cook, stirring, for 3–4 minutes until the onion is soft, then stir in the rice. Cook for a further minute, stirring continuously, then stir in the hot stock.

Cover and simmer gently for 15 minutes, or until the rice has absorbed all the liquid. Cut the eggs into quarters and add half to the mixture with half the parsley.

Carefully fold the cooked fish into the mixture. Season to taste with salt and pepper. Heat the kedgeree through until piping hot.

Transfer the mixture to a large dish and garnish with the remaining quartered eggs and parsley and serve sprinkled with cayenne pepper. Serve immediately.

Russian Fish Pie

Serves 4

350 g/12 oz pollack or whiting fillet
150 ml/¹/₄ pint fish stock
salt and freshly ground
black pepper
50 g/2 oz margarine or butter
1 onion, peeled and finely chopped
50 g/2 oz long-grain rice
1 tbsp freshly chopped dill
50 g/2 oz baby button mushrooms,
quartered
50 g/2 oz peeled prawns,
thawed if frozen
2 medium eggs, hard-boiled
and chopped
450 g/1 lb ready-made puff pastry,
thawed if frozen
plain flour, for dusting
1 small egg, beaten with a pinch
of salt
assorted bitter salad leaves,
to serve

Preheat the oven to 200°C/400°F/Gas Mark 6, 15 minutes before cooking. Place the fish in a shallow frying pan with the stock, 150 ml/¹/₄ pint water and salt and pepper. Simmer for 8–10 minutes. Strain the fish, reserving the cooking liquor and, when cool enough to handle, flake into a bowl.

Melt the margarine or butter in a saucepan and cook the onion for 2–3 minutes, then add the rice, reserved fish liquor and dill. Season lightly. Cover and simmer for 10 minutes, then stir in the mushrooms and cook for a further 10 minutes, or until all the liquid is absorbed. Mix the rice with the cooked fish, prawns and eggs. Leave to cool.

Roll half the pastry out on a lightly floured surface into a 20 x 25 cm/ 8 x 10 inch rectangle. Place on a dampened baking sheet and arrange the fish mixture on top, leaving a 1 cm/¹/₂ inch border.

Roll out the remaining pastry to a rectangle the same size as before and use to cover the fish. Brush the edges lightly with a little of the beaten egg and press to seal. Roll out the pastry trimmings and use to decorate the top. Chill in the refrigerator for 30 minutes. Brush with the beaten egg and bake for 30 minutes, or until golden. Serve immediately with salad leaves.

Salmon Fish Cakes

Serves 4

2 medium tomatoes
350 g/12 oz salmon
fillet, skinned
salt and freshly ground
black pepper
450 g/1 lb potatoes, peeled and
cut into chunks
25 g/1 oz margarine or butter
1 tbsp milk
2 tbsp freshly chopped parsley
75 g/3 oz wholemeal breadcrumbs
2 tbsp plain flour
1 large egg, beaten
3–4 tbsp vegetable oil

To serve:

ready-made raita
fresh mint sprigs

To remove the skins from the tomatoes, pierce each with the tip of a sharp knife, then plunge into boiling water and leave for up to 1 minute. Drain, then rinse in cold water – the skins should peel off easily. Deseed and chop. Reserve.

Place the salmon in a shallow frying pan and cover with water. Season to taste with salt and pepper and simmer for 8–10 minutes until the fish is cooked. Drain and flake into a bowl.

Boil the potatoes in lightly salted water until soft, then drain. Mash with the margarine or butter and milk until smooth. Add the potato to the fish and stir in the tomatoes and half the parsley. Adjust the seasoning to taste. Chill the mixture in the refrigerator for at least 2 hours to firm up.

Mix the breadcrumbs with the remaining parsley. When the fish mixture is firm, form into four flat cakes. First, lightly coat the fish cakes in the flour, then dip into the beaten egg, allowing any excess to drip back into the bowl. Finally, press into the breadcrumb mixture until well coated.

Heat a little of the oil in a frying pan and fry the fish cakes in batches for 2–3 minutes on each side until golden and crisp, adding more oil if necessary. Serve with raita garnished with sprigs of mint.

Fish Crumble

Serves 4

350 g/12 oz whiting or pollack fillets
300 ml/¹/₂ pint milk
salt and freshly ground
black pepper
1 tbsp sunflower oil
75 g/3 oz margarine or butter
1 medium onion, peeled and
finely chopped
2 leeks, trimmed and sliced
1 medium carrot, peeled and
cut into small dice
2 medium potatoes, peeled and
cut into small pieces
175 g/6 oz plain flour
300 ml/¹/₂ pint fish or vegetable stock
1 tsp freshly chopped dill
runner beans, to serve

For the crumble topping:

75 g/3 oz margarine or butter
175 g/6 oz plain flour
25 g/1 oz Parmesan cheese, grated
³/₄ tsp cayenne pepper

Preheat the oven to 200°C/400°F/Gas Mark 6, 15 minutes before cooking. Oil a 1.5 litre/2¹/₂ pint pie dish. Place the fish in a saucepan with the milk, salt and pepper. Bring to the boil, cover and simmer for 8–10 minutes until the fish is cooked. Remove with a slotted spoon, reserving the cooking liquor. Flake the fish into the prepared dish.

Heat the oil and 1 tablespoon of the margarine or butter in a small frying pan and gently fry the onion, leeks, carrot and potatoes for 1–2 minutes. Cover tightly and cook over a gentle heat for a further 10 minutes until softened. Spoon the vegetables over the fish.

Melt the remaining margarine or butter in a saucepan, add the flour and cook for 1 minute, stirring. Whisk in the reserved cooking liquor and the stock. Cook until thickened. Remove from the heat and stir in the dill. Pour over the fish.

To make the crumble, rub the margarine or butter into the flour until it resembles breadcrumbs, then stir in the cheese and cayenne pepper. Sprinkle over the dish and bake in the preheated oven for 20 minutes until piping hot. Serve with runner beans.

Luxury Fish Pasties

Serves 4

75 g/3 oz margarine or butter
75 g/3 oz plain flour
250 ml/8 fl oz milk
175 g/6 oz salmon fillet, skinned
and cut into small pieces
1 tbsp freshly chopped parsley
1 tbsp freshly chopped dill
grated zest and juice of 1 lime
75 g/3 oz peeled prawns,
thawed if frozen
salt and freshly ground
black pepper
350 g/12 oz ready-made puff pastry
1 small egg, beaten
1 tsp sea salt
fresh green salad leaves,
to serve

Preheat the oven to 200°C/400°F/Gas Mark 6. Place the margarine or butter in a saucepan and heat slowly until melted. Add the flour and cook, stirring, for 1 minute. Remove from the heat and gradually add the milk a little at a time, stirring after each addition.

Return to the heat and simmer, stirring continuously, until thickened. Remove from the heat and add the salmon, parsley, dill, lime zest, lime juice, prawns and seasoning.

Roll out the pastry on a lightly floured surface and cut out four 12.5 cm/ 5 inch circles and 4 x 15 cm/6 inch circles. Brush the edges of the smaller circles with the beaten egg and place two tablespoons of the filling in the centre of each one.

Place the larger circles over the filling and press the edges together to seal. Pinch the edge of the pastry between the forefinger and thumb to ensure a firm seal and decorative edge.

Cut a slit in each parcel, brush with the beaten egg and sprinkle with sea salt. Transfer to a baking sheet and cook in the preheated oven for 20 minutes, or until golden brown. Serve immediately with some fresh green salad leaves.

Tuna Fish Burgers

Serves 4

450 g/1 lb potatoes, peeled and
cut into chunks
40 g/1½ oz margarine or butter
2 tbsp milk
400 g can tuna in oil
1 spring onion, trimmed and
finely chopped
1 tbsp freshly chopped parsley
salt and freshly ground
black pepper
2 medium eggs, beaten
2 tbsp seasoned plain flour
125 g/4 oz fresh white breadcrumbs
4 tbsp vegetable oil
4 sesame seed baps (optional)

To serve:

fat chips
mixed salad
tomato chutney

Place the potatoes in a large saucepan, cover with boiling water and simmer until soft. Drain, then mash with the margarine or butter and the milk. Turn into a large bowl. Drain the tuna, discarding the oil, and flake into the bowl of potato. Stir well to mix.

Add the spring onion and parsley and season to taste with salt and pepper. Add 1 tablespoon of the beaten egg to bind the mixture together. Chill in the refrigerator for at least 1 hour.

Shape the chilled mixture with your hands into four large burgers. Coat the burgers with seasoned flour, then brush them with the remaining beaten egg, allowing any excess to drip back into the bowl. Finally, coat them evenly in the breadcrumbs, pressing the crumbs on with your hands if necessary. If possible, cover the uncooked coated burgers with clingfilm and chill in the refrigerator for 30 minutes so that they are really firm.

Heat a little of the oil in a frying pan and fry the burgers for 2–3 minutes on each side until golden, adding more oil if necessary. Drain on kitchen paper and serve hot in baps, if using, with chips, mixed salad and tomato chutney.

Smoked Haddock Rosti

Serves 4

450 g/1 lb potatoes, peeled and
coarsely grated
1 large onion, peeled and
coarsely grated
2–3 garlic cloves, peeled
and crushed
300 g/10 oz smoked haddock
1 tbsp olive oil
salt and freshly ground
black pepper
finely grated zest of ¹/₂ lemon
1 tbsp freshly chopped parsley
2 tbsp crème fraîche
lemon wedges, to serve
mixed salad leaves,
to garnish

Dry the grated potatoes in a clean tea towel. Rinse the grated onion thoroughly in cold water, dry in a clean tea towel and add to the potatoes.

Stir the garlic into the potato mixture. Skin the smoked haddock and remove as many of the tiny pin bones as possible. Cut into thin slices and reserve.

Heat the oil in a nonstick frying pan. Add half the potatoes and press well down in the frying pan. Season to taste with salt and pepper.

Add a layer of fish and a sprinkling of lemon zest, parsley and a little more black pepper.

Top with the remaining potatoes and press down firmly. Cover with a sheet of foil and cook on the lowest heat for 25–30 minutes.

Preheat the grill 2–3 minutes before the end of cooking time. Remove the foil and place the rosti under the grill to brown. Turn out onto a warmed serving dish and serve immediately with spoonfuls of crème fraîche, lemon wedges and mixed salad leaves.

Meat

Meat is a filling and flavoursome ingredient, and a favourite with many. These great recipes show you how to make the most of your meat to produce a tasty meal without the hefty price tag, by focusing on cheaper cuts and versatile ingredients such as sausages and mince. From Chilli Con Carne with Crispy-skinned Potatoes to Bacon and Rigatoni Supper or Oven-roasted Vegetables with Sausages, the recipes in this section are sure to satisfy any meat lover.

Chilli Con Carne with Crispy-skinned Potatoes

Serves 4

1 tbsp vegetable oil, plus extra
for brushing
1 large onion, peeled and
finely chopped
1 garlic clove, peeled and
finely chopped
1 red chilli, deseeded and
finely chopped
350 g/12 oz fresh, lean beef mince
1 tbsp chilli powder
400 g can whole peeled
tomatoes, chopped
2 tbsp tomato purée
400 g can red kidney beans,
drained and rinsed
4 baking potatoes
coarse salt and freshly ground
black pepper

To serve:

ready-made guacamole (optional)
sour cream (optional)

Preheat the oven to 180°C/350°F/Gas Mark 4, 10 minutes before baking. Heat the oil in a large, flameproof casserole dish and add the onion. Cook gently for 10 minutes until soft and lightly browned. Add the garlic and chilli and cook briefly. Increase the heat. Add the mince and cook for a further 10 minutes, stirring occasionally, until browned.

Add the chilli powder and stir well. Cook for about 2 minutes, then add the chopped tomatoes and tomato purée. Bring slowly to the boil, cover and cook in the preheated oven for 1½ hours. Remove from the oven and stir in the kidney beans. Return to the oven for a further 15 minutes.

Meanwhile, brush a little vegetable oil all over the potatoes and rub on some coarse salt. Put the potatoes in the oven alongside the chilli.

Remove the chilli and potatoes from the oven. Cut a cross in each potato, then squeeze to open slightly and season to taste with salt and pepper. Serve with the chilli and, if using, the guacamole and sour cream.

Lamb Biryani

Serves 4

250 g/9 oz basmati rice
4 tbsp vegetable oil
4 whole cloves
4 green cardamom pods, cracked
125 ml/4 fl oz natural yogurt
2 garlic cloves, peeled and crushed
small piece fresh root ginger,
peeled and grated
$^1/_2$ tsp turmeric
2–3 tsp ground coriander
2 tsp ground cumin
350 g/12 oz boneless lean lamb,
such as shoulder, diced
2 onions, peeled and finely sliced
225 g/8 oz tomatoes, chopped
1 tbsp freshly chopped coriander
1 tbsp freshly chopped mint

Rinse the rice at least two or three times, then reserve. Heat 1 tablespoon of the oil in a saucepan, add the cloves and cardamom pods and fry for 30 seconds. Add the rice and cover with boiling water. Bring to the boil, reduce the heat, cover and simmer for 12–15 minutes until the rice is tender. Drain and reserve.

Blend the yogurt, garlic, ginger, turmeric, ground coriander and cumin together with the lamb. Stir, cover and leave to marinate in the refrigerator for at least 2–3 hours.

Preheat the oven to 200°C/400°F/Gas Mark 6, 15 minutes before needed. Heat the remaining oil in a large saucepan, add the onions and fry for 5 minutes, or until softened. Add the tomatoes. Using a slotted spoon, remove the lamb from the marinade, reserving the marinade, and add the lamb to the pan. Cook, stirring, for 5 minutes, then add the remaining marinade. Cover and cook, stirring occasionally, for 25–30 minutes until the lamb is tender and the sauce is thick. Stir in the herbs.

Oil an ovenproof dish. Spoon in a layer of rice and cover with a layer of lamb. Repeat, finishing with a layer of rice. Cover with foil and place in the oven for 10 minutes. Invert onto a warmed plate and serve.

Italian Risotto

ℰ

Serves 4

1 onion, peeled
2 garlic cloves, peeled
1 tbsp olive oil
125 g/4 oz Italian salami or
speck, chopped
125 g/4 oz asparagus spears
350 g/12 oz risotto rice
1.1 litres/2 pints chicken
stock, warmed
125 g/4 oz frozen broad
beans, defrosted
75 g/3 oz Dolcelatte cheese, diced
3 tbsp freshly chopped mixed herbs,
such as parsley and basil
salt and freshly ground
black pepper

Chop the onion and garlic and reserve. Heat the olive oil in a large frying pan and cook the salami for 3–5 minutes until golden. Using a slotted spoon, transfer to a plate and keep warm. Add the asparagus to the pan and stir-fry for 2–3 minutes until just wilted. Transfer to the plate with the salami. Add the onion and garlic to the pan and cook for 5 minutes, or until softened.

Add the rice to the pan and cook for about 2 minutes. Add 300 ml/½ pint of the stock and bring to the boil, then simmer, stirring, until the stock has been absorbed. Add a further 450 ml/¾ pint of the stock and return to the boil. Simmer, stirring, until the liquid has been absorbed.

Add a further 300 ml/¹/₂ pint of the stock and the broad beans to the rice mixture. Bring to the boil, then simmer for a further 5–10 minutes until all of the liquid has been absorbed.

Add the remaining stock, bring to the boil, then simmer until all the liquid is absorbed and the rice is tender. Add the remaining ingredients and stir until the cheese has just melted. Serve immediately.

Lamb ❧ Potato Curry

Serves 4

350 g/12 oz boneless lamb,
such as shoulder
2 tbsp vegetable oil
2 onions, peeled and cut
into wedges
2–3 garlic cloves, peeled and sliced
2 celery stalks, trimmed and sliced
1–2 tbsp Madras curry powder
1 tbsp tomato purée
150 ml/^{1}/$_4$ pint water
150 ml/^{1}/$_4$ pint coconut milk
225 g/8 oz tomatoes, chopped
350 g/12 oz new potatoes, scrubbed
125 g/4 oz carrots, peeled
and sliced

Discard any fat or gristle from the lamb, then cut into thin strips
and reserve.

Heat the oil in a deep frying pan, add the onions, garlic and celery
and fry for 5 minutes, or until softened. Add the curry powder and
continue to fry for a further 2 minutes, stirring constantly. Add the
lamb and cook for 5 minutes, or until coated in the curry paste.

Blend the tomato purée with the water, then stir into the pan
together with the coconut milk and chopped tomatoes.

Cut the potatoes into small chunks and add to the pan with the
carrots. Bring to the boil, then reduce the heat, cover and simmer
for 25–30 minutes until the lamb and vegetables are tender.

Pork Fried Noodles

Serves 4

125 g/4 oz dried thread
egg noodles
125 g/4 oz broccoli florets
2 tbsp groundnut oil
300 g/10 oz pork tenderloin,
cut into slices
3 tbsp soy sauce
1 tbsp lemon juice
pinch sugar
1 tsp chilli sauce
2.5 cm/1 inch piece fresh root
ginger, peeled and cut into sticks
1 garlic clove, peeled
and chopped
1 green chilli, deseeded
and sliced
25 g/1 oz mangetout, halved
2 medium eggs, lightly beaten

To garnish:

radish rose
spring onion curls

Place the noodles in a bowl and cover with boiling water. Leave to stand for 20 minutes, stirring occasionally, or until tender. Drain and reserve. Meanwhile, blanch the broccoli in a saucepan of lightly salted boiling water for 2 minutes. Drain, refresh under cold running water and reserve.

Heat a large wok or frying pan, add the groundnut oil and heat until just smoking. Add the pork and stir-fry for 5 minutes, or until browned. Using a slotted spoon, remove the pork slices and reserve.

Mix together the soy sauce, lemon juice, sugar and chilli sauce; reserve.

Add the ginger to the wok and stir-fry for 30 seconds. Add the garlic and chilli and stir-fry for 30 seconds.

Add the reserved broccoli and stir-fry for 3 minutes. Stir in the mangetout, pork and reserved noodles with the beaten eggs. Stir-fry for 5 minutes, or until heated through. Pour over the reserved sauce, toss well and turn into a warmed serving dish. Garnish and serve immediately.

Cornish Pasties

Serves 4

For the pastry:

225 g/8 oz self-raising flour
50 g/2 oz margarine or butter
50 g/2 oz white vegetable fat
salt and freshly ground
black pepper

For the filling:

225 g/8 oz braising steak,
very finely chopped
1 medium onion, peeled and
finely chopped
1 medium potato, peeled and diced
125 g/4 oz swede, peeled and diced
1–2 tbsp Worcestershire sauce,
or to taste
1 small egg, beaten, to glaze
tomato and parsley, to garnish

Preheat the oven to 180°C/350°F/Gas Mark 4, about 15 minutes before required. To make the pastry, sift the flour into a large bowl and add the fats, chopped into little pieces. Rub the fats and flour together until the mixture resembles coarse breadcrumbs. Season to taste with salt and pepper and mix again.

Add about 1–2 tablespoons cold water, a little at a time, and mix until the mixture comes together to form a firm but pliable dough. Turn onto a lightly floured surface, knead until smooth, then wrap and chill in the refrigerator.

To make the filling, put the steak in a large bowl with the onion. Add the potato and swede to the bowl together with the Worcestershire sauce and salt and pepper. Mix well.

Divide the dough into four balls and roll each ball into a circle about 25 cm/ 10 inches across. Divide the filling between the circles of pastry. Wet the edge of the pastry, then fold over the filling. Pinch the edges to seal.

Transfer the pasties to a lightly oiled baking sheet. Make a couple of small holes in each pasty and brush with beaten egg. Cook in the preheated oven for 15 minutes, remove and brush again with the egg. Return to the oven for a further 15–20 minutes until golden. Cool slightly, garnish with tomato and parsley and serve.

Cassoulet

Serves 4

1 tbsp olive oil
1 onion, peeled and chopped
2 celery stalks, trimmed
and chopped
175 g/6 oz carrots, peeled
and sliced
2–3 garlic cloves, peeled
and crushed
350 g/12 oz pork belly (optional)
8 thick, spicy sausages,
such as Toulouse
few fresh thyme sprigs
salt and freshly ground
black pepper
2 x 400 g cans cannellini beans,
drained and rinsed
600 ml/1 pint vegetable stock
75 g/3 oz fresh breadcrumbs
2 tbsp freshly chopped thyme

Preheat the oven to 180°C/350°F/Gas Mark 4. Heat the oil in a large saucepan or flameproof casserole dish, add the onion, celery, carrots and garlic and sauté for 5 minutes.

Cut the pork, if using, into small pieces and cut the sausages into chunks. Add the meat to the vegetables and cook, stirring, until lightly browned.

Add the thyme sprigs and season to taste with salt and pepper. If a saucepan was used, transfer everything to a casserole dish.

Spoon the beans on top, then pour in the stock. Mix the breadcrumbs with 1 tablespoon of the chopped thyme in a small bowl and sprinkle on top of the beans. Cover with a lid and cook in the preheated oven for 40 minutes. Remove the lid and cook for a further 15 minutes, or until the breadcrumbs are crisp. Sprinkle with the remaining chopped thyme and serve.

Bacon ❧ Rigatoni Supper

Serves 4

25 g/1 oz margarine or butter
2 tbsp olive oil
2 large onions, peeled and
finely sliced
1 tsp soft brown sugar
2 garlic cloves, peeled and crushed
225 g/8 oz streaky bacon, sliced
1 red chilli, deseeded and
finely sliced
400 g can whole peeled
tomatoes, chopped
1 tbsp tomato purée
150 ml/^{1}/$_4$ pint pork or chicken stock
salt and freshly ground
black pepper
450 g/1 lb rigatoni
freshly chopped parsley,
to garnish

Melt the margarine or butter with the olive oil in a large, heavy-based pan. Add the onions and sugar and cook over a very low heat, stirring occasionally, for 15 minutes, or until soft and starting to caramelise.

Add the garlic and bacon to the pan and cook for 5 minutes. Stir in the chilli, chopped tomatoes and tomato purée, then pour in the stock. Season well with salt and pepper. Bring to the boil, cover, reduce the heat and simmer for 30 minutes, stirring occasionally. Remove the lid and simmer for a further 10 minutes, or until the sauce starts to thicken.

Meanwhile, bring a large pan of lightly salted water to a rolling boil. Add the pasta and cook according to the packet instructions, or until *al dente*.

Drain the pasta, reserving 2 tablespoons of the water, and return to the pan. Add the bacon sauce with the reserved cooking water and toss gently until the pasta is evenly covered. Tip into a warmed serving dish, sprinkle with the parsley and serve immediately.

Thai Beef Curry

Serves 4

450 g/1 lb stewing steak
1 tbsp vegetable oil
1–2 tbsp Thai green curry paste,
or to taste
2 onions, peeled and chopped
2 tbsp lime juice
450 ml/³/₄ pint beef stock
150 ml/¹/₄ pint coconut milk
(or 15 g/¹/₂ oz creamed coconut,
chopped, and 150 ml/¹/₄ pint water)
1 tsp soy sauce
1–2 tsp sugar
2 tbsp freshly chopped coriander,
to garnish
freshly cooked egg noodles,
to serve

Trim the beef, discarding any fat and gristle, cut into bite-size chunks and reserve. Heat the oil in a heavy-based saucepan. Add the Thai green curry paste and onions and fry for 5 minutes, or until the onion has begun to soften.

Add the beef to the pan and continue to fry for a further 5 minutes, or until sealed and lightly coated in the paste.

Pour in the lime juice, stock and coconut milk (or chopped creamed coconut dissolved in 150 ml/¹/₂ pint boiling water – or add cold water separately, as it will all have time to mix during the cooking), then add the soy sauce. Stir, then add the sugar. Bring to the boil, reduce the heat, cover and simmer, stirring occasionally, for 2 hours, or until the meat is tender. Check the level of liquid during cooking and, if it is evaporating too quickly, add some more beef stock and reduce the heat. Sprinkle with chopped coriander and serve with freshly cooked noodles.

Singapore Noodles

Serves 4

225 g/8 oz vermicelli rice noodles
2 tbsp vegetable oil
2 shallots, peeled and sliced
2 garlic cloves, peeled and crushed
2 tbsp freshly grated root ginger
1 red pepper, deseeded
and finely sliced
1 red bird's-eye chilli, deseeded
and finely chopped
125 g/4 oz boneless lean pork, diced
125 g/4 oz boneless chicken, diced
1 tbsp curry powder
1 tsp each crushed fennel seeds
and ground cinnamon
125 g/4 oz cooked, peeled prawns,
thawed if frozen
50 g/2 oz frozen peas, thawed
juice of 1 lemon
3 tbsp fresh coriander leaves

Put the noodles into a large bowl and pour over boiling water to cover. Leave to stand for 3 minutes, or until slightly underdone according to the packet instructions. Drain well and reserve.

Heat a wok until almost smoking. Add the oil and carefully swirl around to coat the sides of the wok. Add the shallots, garlic and ginger and cook for a few seconds. Add the pepper and chilli and stir-fry for 3–4 minutes until the pepper has softened.

Add the pork, chicken and curry powder to the wok. Stir-fry for a further 4–5 minutes until the meat is sealed on all sides, then add the fennel seeds and the ground cinnamon and stir to mix.

Add the drained noodles to the wok along with the prawns and peas and cook for a further 2–4 minutes until heated through. Add the lemon juice to taste. Sprinkle with the fresh coriander leaves and serve immediately.

Oven-roasted Vegetables with Sausages

Serves 4

3 tbsp olive oil
1 aubergine, trimmed and cut into
bite-size chunks
3 courgettes, trimmed and cut into
bite-size chunks
6 garlic cloves, unpeeled
8 Tuscany-style sausages
4 plum tomatoes
300 g/10 oz can cannellini beans
salt and freshly ground
black pepper
1 small bunch fresh basil, torn into
coarse pieces
4 tbsp freshly grated Parmesan
cheese

Preheat the oven to 200°C/400°F/Gas Mark 6, 15 minutes before cooking. Line a large roasting tin with foil and pour in the olive oil, then heat in the preheated oven for 3 minutes, or until very hot. Add the aubergine, courgettes and garlic cloves, then stir until coated in the hot oil and cook in the oven for 10 minutes.

Remove the roasting tin from the oven and stir the vegetables. Lightly prick the sausages, add to the roasting tin and return to the oven. Continue to roast for a further 20 minutes, turning once during cooking, until the vegetables are tender and the sausages are golden brown.

Meanwhile, roughly chop the plum tomatoes and drain and rinse the cannellini beans. Remove the roasting tin from the oven and stir in the tomatoes and cannellini beans. Season to taste with salt and pepper, then return to the oven for 5 minutes, or until heated thoroughly.

Scatter over the basil leaves and sprinkle with plenty of Parmesan cheese and freshly ground black pepper. Serve immediately.

Tagliatelle with Creamy Liver & Basil

Serves 4

25 g/1 oz plain flour
salt and freshly ground
black pepper
350 g/12 oz lamb's liver, thinly sliced
and cut into bite-size pieces
25 g/1 oz margarine or butter
1 tbsp olive oil
2 red onions, peeled and sliced
1 garlic clove, peeled and sliced
150 ml/¼ pint chicken stock
1 tbsp tomato purée
2 tomatoes, finely chopped
350 g/12 oz tagliatelle verdi
1 tbsp freshly chopped basil
150 ml/¼ pint single cream
fresh basil leaves, to garnish

Season the flour lightly with salt and pepper and place in a large plastic bag. Add the liver and toss gently to coat. Remove the liver from the bag and reserve.

Melt the margarine or butter with the olive oil in a large frying pan. Add the onions and garlic and fry for 6–8 minutes until the onions begin to colour. Add the liver and fry until brown on all sides.

Stir in the chicken stock, tomato purée and tomatoes. Bring to the boil, reduce the heat and simmer very gently for 10 minutes.

Meanwhile, bring a large pan of lightly salted water to a rolling boil. Add the pasta and cook according to the packet instructions, or until *al dente*.

Stir the chopped basil and the cream into the liver sauce and season to taste.

Drain the pasta thoroughly, reserving 2 tablespoons of the cooking water. Tip the pasta into a warmed serving dish or pile onto individual plates. Stir the reserved cooking water into the liver sauce and pour over the pasta. Toss lightly to coat the pasta. Garnish with basil leaves and serve immediately.

Cannelloni with Spicy Bolognese Filling

Serves 4

8 dried cannelloni tubes
300 ml/^{1}/$_2$ pint prepared white sauce
25 g/1 oz freshly grated
Parmesan cheese
^{1}/$_4$ tsp freshly grated nutmeg
crisp green salad, to serve

For the spicy Bolognese filling:

1 tbsp olive oil
1 small onion, peeled and
finely chopped
2 garlic cloves, peeled and crushed
350 g/12 oz fresh, lean beef mince
^{1}/$_4$ tsp crushed chilli flakes
2 tbsp freshly chopped oregano
400 g can whole peeled
tomatoes, chopped
1 tbsp tomato purée
150 ml/^{1}/$_4$ pint beef stock
salt and freshly ground black pepper

Preheat the oven to 200°C/400°F/Gas Mark 6, 15 minutes before cooking the stuffed cannelloni. For the filling, heat the oil in a large, heavy-based pan, add the onion and garlic and cook for 8 minutes, or until soft. Add the beef mince and cook, stirring with a wooden spoon to break up lumps, for 5–8 minutes until the meat is browned.

Stir in the chilli flakes, oregano, tomatoes and tomato purée and pour in the stock. Season to taste with salt and pepper. Bring to the boil, cover with a lid and lower the heat, then simmer for at least 30 minutes, stirring occasionally. Remove the lid and simmer for a further 10 minutes. Allow to cool slightly.

Using a teaspoon, fill the cannelloni tubes with the meat filling. Lay the stuffed cannelloni side by side in a lightly oiled ovenproof dish.

Pour the prepared white sauce over the cannelloni tubes and sprinkle with the Parmesan cheese and the nutmeg. Bake in the preheated oven for 30 minutes, or until golden brown and bubbling. Serve immediately with a green salad.

Lamb with Black Cherry Sauce

Serves 4

450 g/1 lb lamb fillet
2 tbsp light soy sauce
1 tsp Chinese five-spice powder
4 tbsp fresh orange juice
125 g/4 oz black cherry jam
150 ml/^{1}/$_4$ pint chicken stock
50 g/2 oz fresh black cherries
1 tbsp groundnut oil
1 tbsp freshly chopped coriander,
to garnish

To serve:

freshly cooked peas
freshly cooked noodles

Remove the skin and any fat from the lamb fillet and cut into thin slices. Place in a shallow dish. Mix together the soy sauce, Chinese five-spice powder and orange juice and pour over the meat. Cover and leave in the refrigerator for at least 30 minutes.

Meanwhile, blend the jam and the stock together, pour into a small saucepan and bring to the boil. Simmer gently for 10 minutes until slightly thickened. Remove the stones from the fresh cherries, using a cherry stoner if possible in order to keep them whole. Add the cherries to the sauce.

Drain the lamb when ready to cook. Heat the wok, add the oil and, when the oil is hot, stir-fry the slices of lamb for 3–5 minutes until just slightly pink inside or cooked to personal preference.

Spoon the lamb into a warmed serving dish and drizzle with a little of the cherry sauce. Garnish with the chopped coriander and the whole cherries and serve immediately with peas, freshly cooked noodles and the remaining sauce.

Pork Sausages with Onion Gravy & Mash

Serves 4

3 tbsp olive oil
2 large onions, peeled and
thinly sliced
pinch sugar
1 tbsp freshly chopped thyme
1 tbsp plain flour
300 ml/¹/₂ pint vegetable stock
8–12 good-quality butcher's pork
sausages, depending on size

For the mash:

700 g/1¹/₂ lb floury potatoes, peeled
25 g/1 oz margarine or butter
4 tbsp crème fraîche or sour cream
salt and freshly ground
black pepper

Heat the oil and add the onions. Cover and cook gently for about 20 minutes until the onions have collapsed. Add the sugar and stir well. Uncover and continue to cook, stirring often, until the onions are very soft and golden. Add the thyme, stir well, then add the flour, stirring. Gradually add the stock. Bring to the boil and simmer gently for 10 minutes.

Meanwhile, put the sausages in a large frying pan and cook over a medium heat for about 15–20 minutes, turning often, until golden brown and slightly sticky all over.

For the mash, boil the potatoes in plenty of lightly salted water for 15–18 minutes until tender. Drain well and return to the saucepan. Put the saucepan over a low heat to allow the potatoes to dry thoroughly. Remove from the heat and add the margarine or butter, crème fraîche or sour cream and salt and pepper. Mash thoroughly. Serve the potato mash with the sausages and onion gravy.

Moroccan Penne

1 tbsp sunflower oil
1 red onion, peeled and chopped
2 garlic cloves, peeled and crushed
1 tbsp coriander seeds
$^1/_4$ tsp cumin seeds
$^1/_4$ tsp freshly grated nutmeg
450 g/1 lb fresh, lean lamb mince
1 aubergine, trimmed and diced
400 g can whole peeled
tomatoes, chopped
300 ml/$^1/_2$ pint vegetable stock
125 g/4 oz ready-to-eat
apricots, chopped
12 pitted black olives
salt and freshly ground
black pepper
350 g/12 oz penne
1 tbsp toasted pine nuts, to garnish
(optional)

Preheat the oven to 200°C/400°F/Gas Mark 6, 15 minutes before cooking. Heat the sunflower oil in a large, flameproof casserole dish. Add the onion and fry for 5 minutes, or until softened.

Using a pestle and mortar, pound the garlic, coriander seeds, cumin seeds and grated nutmeg together into a paste. Add to the onion and cook for 3 minutes.

Add the lamb mince to the casserole dish and fry, stirring with a wooden spoon, for 4–5 minutes until the mince has broken up and browned.

Add the aubergine to the mince and fry for 5 minutes. Stir in the chopped tomatoes and vegetable stock and bring to the boil. Add the apricots and olives, then season well with salt and pepper. Return to the boil, lower the heat and simmer for 15 minutes.

Add the penne to the casserole dish, stir well, then cover and place in the preheated oven. Cook for 10 minutes, then stir and return to the oven, uncovered, for a further 15–20 minutes until the pasta is *al dente*. Remove from the oven, sprinkle with toasted pine nuts, if using, and serve immediately.

Spaghetti & Meatballs

Serves 4

400 g can chopped tomatoes
1 tbsp tomato paste
1 tsp chilli sauce
1/4 tsp brown sugar
salt and freshly ground
black pepper
350 g/12 oz spaghetti
75g/3 oz Cheddar cheese, grated, plus
extra to serve
freshly chopped parsley, to garnish

For the meatballs:

450 g/1 lb lean pork or beef mince
125 g/4 oz fresh breadcrumbs
1 large onion, peeled and
finely chopped
1 medium egg, beaten
1 tbsp tomato paste
2 tbsp freshly chopped parsley
1 tbsp freshly chopped oregano

Preheat the oven to 200˚C/400˚F/Gas Mark 6, 15 minutes before using. Place the chopped tomatoes, tomato paste, chilli sauce and sugar in a saucepan. Season to taste with salt and pepper and bring to the boil. Cover and simmer for 15 minutes, then cook, uncovered, for a further 10 minutes, or until the sauce has reduced and thickened.

Meanwhile, make the meatballs. Place the meat, breadcrumbs and onion in a food processor. Blend until all the ingredients are well mixed. Add the beaten egg, tomato paste, parsley and oregano and season to taste. Blend again.

Shape the mixture into small balls, about the size of an apricot, and place on an oiled baking tray. Cook in the preheated oven for 25–30 minutes, or until browned and cooked.

Meanwhile, bring a large pan of lightly salted water to a rolling boil. Add the pasta and cook according to the packet instructions, or until *al dente*.

Drain the pasta and return to the pan. Pour over the tomato sauce and toss gently to coat the spaghetti. Tip into a warmed serving dish and top with the meatballs. Garnish with chopped parsley and serve immediately with grated cheese.

Lamb Balti

Serves 4

350 g/12 oz lamb, such as boneless
shoulder or neck fillet, trimmed
2 tbsp vegetable oil
1–2 tbsp ready-made
balti paste
2–3 garlic cloves, peeled
and crushed
2–3 green chillies, deseeded
and chopped
2 onions, peeled and chopped
1 aubergine, trimmed and chopped
4 tomatoes, chopped
2 tsp tomato purée
600 ml/1 pint lamb or
vegetable stock
2 tbsp freshly chopped coriander
naan bread, to serve

Dice the lamb and reserve. Heat the oil in a large frying pan, add the balti paste and fry for 30 seconds.

Add the garlic, chillies, onions and aubergine. Cook, stirring, for a further 5 minutes, or until the vegetables are coated in the paste.

Add the lamb and continue to fry for 5–8 minutes until sealed. Stir in the chopped tomatoes.

Blend the tomato purée with the stock, then pour into the pan. Bring to the boil, cover, reduce the heat and simmer for 45–50 minutes until the lamb is tender. Sprinkle with chopped coriander and serve with plenty of naan bread.

Cottage Pie

Serves 4

350 g/12 oz fresh, lean beef mince
2 tbsp vegetable or olive oil
1 onion, peeled and
finely chopped
1 carrot, peeled and
finely chopped
1 celery stalk, trimmed and
finely chopped
1 tbsp fresh thyme leaves
300 ml/$^1/_2$ pint beef or vegetable
stock or leftover gravy
2 tbsp tomato purée
salt and freshly ground
black pepper
700 g/1$^1/_2$ lb potatoes, peeled and
cut into chunks
25 g/1 oz margarine or butter
6 tbsp milk
1 tbsp freshly chopped parsley
fresh herbs, to garnish

Preheat the oven to 200°C/400°F/Gas Mark 6, about 15 minutes before cooking. Place the beef mince in a frying pan and place over a medium heat. Cook, stirring frequently, until browned. Spoon into a colander or sieve to allow any fat to be discarded. Reserve the mince.

Wipe the frying pan clean, then heat the oil and add the onion, carrot and celery. Cook over a medium heat for 8–10 minutes until softened and starting to brown. Add the thyme and cook briefly, then return the beef mince to the pan together with the stock or gravy and tomato purée. Season to taste with salt and pepper and simmer gently for 25–30 minutes until reduced and thickened. Remove from the heat to cool slightly and check the seasoning.

Meanwhile, boil the potatoes in plenty of salted water for 12–15 minutes until tender. Drain and return to the saucepan over a low heat to dry out. Remove from the heat and add the margarine or butter, milk and parsley. Mash until creamy, adding a little more milk if necessary. Adjust the seasoning.

Transfer the beef mixture to a shallow, ovenproof dish. Spoon the mash over the filling and spread evenly to cover completely. Fork the surface, place on a baking sheet, then cook in the preheated oven for 25–30 minutes until the potato topping is browned and the filling is piping hot. Garnish and serve.

Braised Lamb with Broad Beans

Serves 4

350 g/12 oz shoulder or neck
of lamb, diced
1 tbsp plain flour
1 onion
2 garlic cloves
1 tbsp olive oil
400 g can whole peeled
tomatoes, chopped
300 ml/^{1}/$_2$ pint lamb or chicken stock
2 tbsp freshly chopped oregano
salt and freshly ground
black pepper
225 g/8 oz frozen broad beans
fresh oregano, to garnish
creamy mashed potatoes,
to serve

Trim the lamb, discarding any fat or gristle, then place the flour in a polythene bag, add the lamb and toss until coated thoroughly. Peel and slice the onion and garlic and reserve. Heat the olive oil in a heavy-based saucepan and, when hot, add the lamb and cook, stirring, until the meat is sealed and browned all over. Using a slotted spoon, transfer the lamb to a plate and reserve.

Add the onion and garlic to the saucepan and cook for 3 minutes, stirring frequently until softened, then return the lamb to the saucepan. Add the chopped tomatoes with their juice, the stock and the chopped oregano and season to taste with salt and pepper. Bring to the boil, then cover with a close-fitting lid, reduce the heat and simmer for 1 hour.

Add the broad beans to the lamb and simmer for 20–30 minutes until the lamb is tender. Garnish with fresh oregano and serve with creamy mashed potatoes.

Tagliatelle with Spicy Sausage Ragù

Serves 4

3 tbsp olive oil
4 spicy sausages
1 small onion, peeled and
finely chopped
1–2 garlic cloves, peeled
and crushed
1 tsp fennel seeds
175 g/6 oz fresh pork mince
225 g/8 oz canned whole, peeled
tomatoes, chopped, plus 2 tbsp
of the tomato liquor
1 tbsp tomato purée
salt and freshly ground
black pepper
350 g/12 oz tagliatelle
300 ml/¹/₂ pint prepared white sauce
25 g/1 oz freshly grated
Parmesan cheese

Preheat the oven to 200°C/400°F/Gas Mark 6, 15 minutes before baking. Heat 1 tablespoon of the olive oil in a large frying pan. Prick the sausages, add to the pan and cook for 8–10 minutes until browned and cooked through. Remove and cut into thin diagonal slices. Reserve.

Return the pan to the heat and pour in the remaining olive oil. Add the onion and garlic and cook for 8 minutes, or until softened. Add the fennel seeds and pork mince and cook, stirring, for 5–8 minutes until the meat is sealed and browned.

Stir in the tomatoes with their liquor and the tomato purée. Season to taste with salt and pepper. Bring to the boil, cover and simmer for 30 minutes, stirring occasionally. Remove the lid and simmer for 10 minutes.

Bring a large pan of lightly salted water to a rolling boil. Add the pasta and cook according to the packet instructions, or until *al dente*. Drain thoroughly and toss with the meat sauce.

Place half the pasta in an ovenproof dish and cover with 4 tablespoons of the white sauce. Top with half the sausages and grated Parmesan cheese. Repeat the layering, finishing with white sauce and Parmesan cheese. Bake in the preheated oven for 20 minutes until golden brown. Serve immediately.

Chilli Beef Calzone

Serves 4

For the basic pizza dough:

225 g/8 oz strong plain flour
1/2 tsp salt
1/4 tsp quick-acting dried yeast
150 ml/1/4 pint warm water
1 tbsp olive oil

For the filling:

1 tbsp sunflower oil
1 onion, peeled and finely chopped
1 green pepper, deseeded
and chopped
225 g/8 oz fresh lean beef mince
420 g can chilli beans
200 g/7 oz whole canned
tomatoes, chopped
mixed salad leaves, to serve

Preheat the oven to 220°C/425°F/Gas Mark 7, 15 minutes before baking. Sift the flour and salt into a bowl and stir in the yeast. Make a well in the centre and gradually add the water and oil to form a soft dough.

Knead the dough on a floured surface for about 5 minutes until smooth and elastic. Place in a lightly oiled bowl and cover with clingfilm. Leave to rise in a warm place for 1 hour.

Heat the oil in a large saucepan and gently cook the onion and pepper for 5 minutes. Add the beef mince to the saucepan and cook for 10 minutes until browned. Add the chilli beans and tomatoes and simmer gently for 30 minutes, or until the mince is tender. Place a baking sheet into the preheated oven to heat up.

Knock the pizza dough with your fist a few times, then divide into four equal pieces. Cover three pieces of the dough with clingfilm and roll out the other piece on a lightly floured board to a 20.5 cm/8 inch round.

Spoon a quarter of the chilli mixture onto half of the dough round and dampen the edges with a little water. Fold over the empty half of the dough and press the edges together well to seal. Repeat this process with the remaining dough. Place on the hot baking sheet and bake for 15 minutes. Serve with the salad leaves.

Poultry

Just because poultry is inexpensive doesn't mean it needs to be boring! This section features a great many spicy dishes and curries, such as Spicy Mexican Chicken and Stir-fried Chinese Chicken Curry. If fiery foods aren't to your taste, never fear – there are also milder recipes such as Chicken & Ham Pie and Cheesy Chicken Burgers.

Penne with Pan-fried Chicken & Capers

Serves 4

350 g/12 oz boneless, skinless
chicken thighs
25 g/1 oz plain flour
salt and freshly ground
black pepper
350 g/12 oz penne
2 tbsp olive oil
1 red onion, peeled and sliced
1 garlic clove, peeled and chopped
2–4 tbsp pesto
200 g/7 oz cream cheese
1 tsp wholegrain mustard
1 tbsp lemon juice
2 tbsp freshly chopped basil
1 tbsp capers in brine, rinsed
and drained
freshly shaved Pecorino Romano
cheese, to serve

Trim the chicken and cut into bite-size pieces. Season the flour with salt and pepper, then toss the chicken in the seasoned flour and reserve.

Bring a large saucepan of lightly salted water to a rolling boil. Add the penne and cook according to the packet instructions, or until *al dente*.

Meanwhile, heat the olive oil in a large frying pan. Add the chicken to the pan and cook for 8 minutes, or until golden on all sides, stirring frequently. Transfer the chicken to a plate and reserve.

Add the onion and garlic to the oil remaining in the frying pan and cook for 5 minutes, or until softened, stirring frequently.

Return the chicken to the frying pan. Stir in the pesto and cream cheese and heat through, stirring gently, until smooth. Stir in the wholegrain mustard, lemon juice, basil and capers. Season to taste, then continue to heat through until piping hot.

Drain the penne thoroughly and return to the saucepan. Pour over the sauce and toss well to coat. Arrange the pasta on individual warmed plates. Scatter with the cheese and serve immediately.

North Indian Slow-cooked Chicken

Serves 4

8 small chicken thighs
3–4 tbsp vegetable oil
2 onions, peeled and cut
into wedges
2–3 garlic cloves, peeled and sliced
1 green chilli, deseeded and sliced
1 red chilli, deseeded and sliced
2–3 tbsp Madras curry paste,
or to taste
450 ml/³/₄ pint water
2 tbsp lemon juice
2 tbsp sesame seeds
freshly cooked rice, to serve
fresh coriander sprigs,
to garnish

Lightly rinse the chicken and pat dry with absorbent kitchen paper. Heat 2 tablespoons of the oil in a large, deep frying pan, add the chicken and brown on all sides. Remove and reserve.

Add a further tablespoon of the oil to the pan if necessary, then add the onions, garlic and half the chillies and fry for 5 minutes, or until beginning to soften. Stir in the curry paste and cook for 2 minutes, stirring frequently. Take care not to burn the mixture.

Take off the heat, return the chicken to the pan and roll around in the paste until lightly coated. Stir in the water. Return to the heat and bring to the boil. Reduce the heat, cover and simmer for 35 minutes, or until the chicken is tender. Pour the lemon juice over the chicken and cook for a further 10 minutes.

Meanwhile, heat the remaining oil in a small frying pan and gently fry the rest of the chillies and the sesame seeds until the chillies have become crisp and the seeds are toasted.

Serve the chicken on a bed of rice, sprinkled with the crispy chillies and toasted sesame seeds and garnished with coriander sprigs.

Turkey ❧ Mixed Mushroom Lasagne

Serves 4

1 tbsp olive oil
225 g/8 oz mixed mushrooms, e.g.
button, chestnut and portobello,
wiped and sliced
15 g/¹/₂ oz margarine or butter
25 g/1 oz plain flour
300 ml/¹/₂ pint milk
1 bay leaf
225 g/8 oz cooked
turkey, cubed
¹/₄ tsp freshly grated nutmeg
salt and freshly ground
black pepper
400 g can whole peeled tomatoes,
drained and chopped
1 tsp dried mixed herbs
9 lasagne sheets (about 150 g/5 oz)
mixed salad leaves, to serve

For the topping:

200 ml/7 fl oz Greek yogurt
1 medium egg, lightly beaten
1 tbsp finely grated Parmesan cheese

Preheat the oven to 180°C/350°F/Gas Mark 4. Heat the oil and cook the mushrooms until tender and all the juices have evaporated. Remove and reserve.

Put the margarine or butter, flour, milk and bay leaf in the pan. Slowly bring to the boil, stirring until thickened. Simmer for 2–3 minutes. Remove the bay leaf and stir in the mushrooms, turkey, nutmeg, salt and pepper.

Mix together the tomatoes and mixed herbs and season with salt and pepper. Spoon half into the base of a 1.7 litre/3 pint ovenproof dish. Top with 3 lasagne sheets, then with half the turkey mixture. Repeat (a layer of tomatoes, a layer of pasta, a layer of turkey), then arrange the remaining 3 pasta sheets on top.

Mix together the yogurt and egg. Spoon over the lasagne, spreading the mixture into the corners. Sprinkle with the grated cheese.

Cook in the preheated oven for 40–45 minutes until the top is golden brown and bubbling. Serve with a green salad.

Spicy Mexican Chicken

Serves 4

2 tbsp olive oil
350 g/12 oz fresh chicken mince
1 red onion, peeled and chopped
2 garlic cloves, peeled and chopped
1 red pepper, deseeded
and chopped
1–2 tsp hot chilli powder
2 tbsp tomato purée
225 ml/8 fl oz chicken stock
salt and freshly ground
black pepper
200 g/7 oz can red kidney beans,
drained
200 g/7 oz canned chilli beans,
drained
350 g/12 oz spaghetti

To serve (optional):
Cheddar cheese, grated
guacamole
hot chilli salsa

Heat the oil in a large frying pan, add the chicken mince and cook for 5 minutes, stirring frequently with a wooden spoon to break up any lumps. Add the onion, garlic and pepper and cook for 3 minutes. Stir in the chilli powder and cook for a further 2 minutes.

Stir in the tomato purée, then pour in the chicken stock and season to taste with salt and pepper. Bring to the boil, reduce the heat and simmer, covered, for 20 minutes.

Add the kidney and chilli beans and cook, stirring occasionally, for 10 minutes, or until the chicken is tender.

Meanwhile, bring a large pan of lightly salted water to a rolling boil. Add the spaghetti and cook according to the packet instructions, or until *al dente*.

Drain the spaghetti thoroughly, arrange on warmed plates and spoon over the chicken and bean mixture. Serve with the grated cheese, guacamole and salsa, if using.

Spaghetti with Turkey & Bacon Sauce

Serves 4

350 g/12 oz spaghetti
25 g/1 oz margarine or butter
125 g/4 oz smoked streaky bacon,
rind removed
225 g/8 oz fresh turkey
breast strips
1 onion, peeled and chopped
1 garlic clove, peeled and chopped
3 medium eggs, beaten
300 ml/½ pint single cream
salt and freshly ground
black pepper
25 g/1 oz freshly grated Cheddar or
Parmesan cheese
2–3 tbsp freshly chopped coriander,
to garnish (optional)

Bring a large pan of lightly salted water to a rolling boil. Add the spaghetti and cook according to the packet instructions, or until *al dente*.

Meanwhile, melt the margarine or butter in a large frying pan. Using a sharp knife, finely slice the streaky bacon. Add the bacon to the pan with the turkey strips and cook for 8 minutes, or until browned, stirring occasionally to prevent sticking. Add the onion and garlic and cook for 5 minutes, or until softened, stirring occasionally.

Place the eggs and cream in a bowl and season to taste with salt and pepper. Beat together, then pour into the frying pan and cook, stirring, for 2 minutes, or until the mixture begins to thicken but does not scramble. (It is a good idea to remove the pan from the heat before adding the beaten eggs to the pan, as there should be enough residual heat in the sauce to cook them. If the sauce does not start to thicken after 2 minutes, return to the heat and cook for 1–2 more minutes.)

Drain the spaghetti thoroughly and return to the pan. Pour over the sauce, add the grated cheese and toss lightly. Heat through for 2 minutes, or until piping hot. Tip into a warmed serving dish and sprinkle with freshly chopped coriander, if using. Serve immediately.

Cheesy Chicken Burgers

Serves 4

1 tbsp sunflower oil
1 small onion, peeled and finely chopped
1 garlic clove, peeled and crushed
$1/2$ red pepper, deseeded and
finely chopped
350 g/12 oz fresh chicken mince
2 tbsp Greek yogurt
40 g/1$1/2$ oz fresh brown breadcrumbs
1 tbsp freshly chopped herbs, such
as parsley or tarragon
50 g/2 oz Cheshire cheese, crumbled
salt and freshly ground black pepper

For the sweetcorn and carrot relish:

125 g/4 oz canned sweetcorn, drained
1 small carrot, peeled and grated
$1/2$ green chilli, deseeded and
finely chopped
2 tsp white wine vinegar
2 tsp soft light brown sugar

To serve:

wholemeal or granary rolls; lettuce;
sliced tomatoes; mixed salad leaves

Preheat the grill to medium. Heat the oil in a frying pan and gently cook the onion and garlic for 5 minutes. Add the red pepper and cook for 5 minutes. Transfer into a mixing bowl and add the chicken, yogurt, breadcrumbs, herbs and cheese and season to taste with salt and pepper. Mix well. Divide the mixture equally into six and shape into burgers. Cover and chill in the refrigerator for at least 20 minutes.

To make the relish, put all the ingredients in a small saucepan with 1 tablespoon water and heat gently, stirring occasionally, until all the sugar has dissolved. Cover and cook over a low heat for 2 minutes, then uncover and cook for a further minute, or until the relish is thick.

Place the burgers on a lightly oiled grill pan and cook under the preheated grill for 8–10 minutes on each side until browned and completely cooked through.

Warm the rolls, if liked, then split in half and fill with the burgers, lettuce, sliced tomatoes and the prepared relish. Serve with mixed salad leaves.

Chicken ❧ Chickpea Korma

Serves 4

350 g/12 oz skinless, boneless
chicken, such as thighs
2 tbsp vegetable oil
2 onions, peeled and cut
into wedges
2–4 garlic cloves, peeled
and chopped
2–3 tbsp Korma curry paste
450 ml/³/₄ pint chicken stock
225 g/8 oz ripe tomatoes, peeled
and chopped
400 g can chickpeas, drained
and rinsed
4 tbsp single cream
6 spring onions, trimmed and
diagonally sliced
Indian-style bread, to serve

Cut the chicken into small strips and reserve. Heat the oil in a wok or frying pan, add the chicken and cook, stirring, for 3 minutes, or until sealed. Remove and reserve.

Add the onions and garlic to the pan and fry gently for 5 minutes, or until the onion has begun to soften. Add the curry paste and cook, stirring, for 2 minutes. Return the chicken to the pan and stir well.

Add the stock, tomatoes and chickpeas, then bring to the boil, reduce and simmer for 15–20 minutes until the chicken is cooked. Stir in the cream. Spoon into a warmed serving dish, sprinkle with the spring onions and serve with Indian-style bread.

Bengali Chicken Curry

Serves 4

2–3 red chillies, deseeded
and chopped
3 garlic cloves, peeled and chopped
5 cm/2 inch piece root ginger,
peeled and grated
4 shallots, peeled and chopped
1 tsp turmeric
1–2 tsp curry powder
250 ml/8 fl oz water
350 g/12 oz skinless, boneless
chicken, such as thighs
2 tbsp vegetable oil
1 tbsp freshly chopped coriander

To serve:

Indian-style bread
salad

Place the chillies, garlic, ginger, shallots, turmeric, curry powder and 150 ml/¼ pint of the water in a food processor until smooth, then reserve until required.

Lightly rinse the chicken and pat dry with absorbent kitchen paper. Cut the chicken into thin strips, then place in a shallow dish and pour over the spice mixture. Cover and leave to marinate in the refrigerator for 15–30 minutes, stirring occasionally.

Heat the oil in a heavy-based frying pan, then, using a slotted spoon, remove the chicken from the marinade, reserving the marinade. Cook the chicken for 10 minutes, or until sealed.

Remove the chicken and reserve. Pour the reserved marinade into the pan and cook gently for 2 minutes. Return the chicken to the pan together with the remaining water. Bring to the boil, then reduce the heat and simmer for 15 minutes, stirring occasionally, until the chicken is cooked. Spoon into a warmed serving dish, sprinkle with the chopped coriander and serve with bread and salad.

Chicken Marengo

Serves 4

2 tbsp plain flour
salt and freshly ground
black pepper
4 skinless, boneless chicken thighs,
cut into bite-size pieces
3 tbsp olive oil
1 large onion, peeled and chopped
1 garlic clove, peeled and chopped
400 g can whole peeled tomatoes,
chopped
2 tbsp tomato purée
1 tbsp freshly chopped basil
1–2 tsp dried thyme
125 ml/4 fl oz chicken stock
350 g/12 oz rigatoni
3 tbsp freshly chopped
flat-leaf parsley (optional)

Season the flour with salt and pepper and toss the chicken in the flour to coat. Heat 2 tablespoons of the olive oil in a large frying pan and cook the chicken for 7 minutes, or until browned all over, turning occasionally. Remove from the pan using a slotted spoon, and keep warm.

Add the remaining oil to the pan, add the onion and cook, stirring occasionally, for 5 minutes, or until softened and starting to brown. Add the garlic, tomatoes, tomato purée, basil and thyme. Pour in the chicken stock and season well. Bring to the boil. Stir in the chicken pieces and simmer for 15 minutes, or until the chicken is tender and the sauce has thickened.

Meanwhile, bring a large pan of lightly salted water to a rolling boil. Add the rigatoni and cook according to the packet instructions, or until *al dente*.

Drain the rigatoni thoroughly, return to the pan and stir in the chopped parsley, if using. Tip the pasta into a large warmed serving dish or spoon onto individual plates. Spoon over the chicken sauce and serve immediately.

Turkey Hash with Potato & Beetroot

Serves 4

2 tbsp vegetable oil
50 g/2 oz margarine or butter
4 slices streaky bacon, rind and cartilage removed, then diced or sliced
1 onion, peeled and finely chopped
350 g/12 oz cooked turkey meat, diced
450 g/1 lb cooked potatoes, sliced
2–3 tbsp freshly chopped parsley
2 tbsp plain flour
250 g/9 oz cooked beetroot (not in vinegar), diced
green salad, to serve

In a large, heavy-based frying pan, heat the oil and half the margarine or butter over a medium heat until sizzling. Add the bacon and cook for 4 minutes, or until crisp and golden, stirring occasionally. Using a slotted spoon, transfer to a large bowl. Add the onion to the pan and cook for 5–8 minutes until soft and golden, stirring frequently.

Meanwhile, add the turkey, potatoes, parsley and flour to the cooked bacon in the bowl. Stir and toss gently, then fold in the diced beetroot.

Add half the remaining margarine or butter to the frying pan and then the turkey and vegetable mixture. Stir, then spread the mixture to cover the bottom of the frying pan evenly. Cook for 15 minutes, or until the underside is crisp and brown, pressing the hash firmly into a cake with a spatula. Remove from the heat.

Invert a large plate over the frying pan and, holding the plate and frying pan together with an oven glove, turn the hash out onto the plate. Heat the remaining margarine or butter in the pan, slide the hash back into the pan and cook for 4 minutes, or until crisp and brown on the other side. Invert onto the plate again and serve immediately with a green salad.

Thai Chicken Fried Rice

Serves 4

175 g/6 oz chicken breast fillets
2 tbsp vegetable oil
2 garlic cloves, peeled and
finely chopped
2–3 tsp Thai red curry paste,
or to taste
450 g/1 lb cold cooked rice
1 tbsp light soy sauce
2 tbsp Thai fish sauce
large pinch sugar
freshly ground black pepper

To garnish:

2 spring onions, trimmed and
shredded lengthways
1/2 small onion, peeled and very
finely sliced

Using a sharp knife, trim the chicken, discarding any skin, sinew or fat, and cut into small cubes. Reserve.

Heat a wok or large frying pan, add the oil and, when hot, add the garlic and cook for 10–20 seconds until just golden. Add the curry paste and stir-fry for a few seconds. Add the chicken and stir-fry for 3–4 minutes until tender and the chicken has turned white.

Stir the cold cooked rice into the chicken mixture, then add the soy sauce, fish sauce and sugar, stirring well after each addition. Cook, stirring, for 5–8 minutes until the chicken is cooked through and the rice is piping hot.

Check the seasoning and, if necessary, add a little extra soy sauce. Turn the rice and chicken mixture into a warmed serving dish. Season lightly with black pepper and garnish with shredded spring onions and onion slices. Serve immediately.

Spiced Indian Roast Potatoes with Chicken

Serves 4

450 g/1 lb waxy potatoes, peeled
and cut into large chunks
4 tbsp sunflower oil
8 small chicken drumsticks
1 large onion, peeled and
roughly chopped
2 large garlic cloves, peeled
and crushed
1 red chilli
2 tsp fresh root ginger, peeled and
finely grated
2 tsp ground cumin
2 tsp ground coriander
pinch cayenne pepper
salt and freshly ground
black pepper
4 cardamom pods, crushed
fresh coriander sprigs,
to garnish

Preheat the oven to 190°C/375°F/Gas Mark 5, about 10 minutes before cooking. Parboil the potatoes for 5 minutes in lightly salted boiling water, then drain thoroughly and reserve. Heat the oil in a large frying pan, add the chicken drumsticks and cook until sealed on all sides. Remove and reserve.

Add the onion to the pan and fry for 4–5 minutes until softened. Stir in the garlic, chilli and ginger and cook for 1 minute, stirring constantly. Stir in the ground cumin, coriander, cayenne pepper and crushed cardamom pods and continue to cook, stirring, for a further minute.

Add the potatoes to the pan, then add the chicken drumsticks. Season to taste with salt and pepper. Stir gently until the potatoes and chicken are coated in the onion and spice mixture.

Spoon into a large roasting tin and roast in the preheated oven for 35 minutes, or until the chicken and potatoes are cooked thoroughly. Garnish with fresh coriander and serve immediately.

Stir-fried Chinese Chicken Curry

Serves 4

350 g/12 oz skinless, boneless
chicken, such as thighs
1 egg white
1 tsp salt
1 tbsp cornflour
2 tbsp groundnut oil
225 g/8 oz carrots, peeled and cut
into very thin batons
1 large red pepper, deseeded and
cut into thin strips
1 large green pepper, deseeded
and cut into thin strips
1–2 tbsp curry paste
175–200 ml/6–7 fl oz chicken stock
1 tbsp rice wine or white
wine vinegar
1 tsp demerara sugar
1 tbsp light soy sauce
6 spring onions, trimmed and
diagonally sliced
freshly cooked sticky rice,
to serve

Cut the chicken into small, bite-size pieces and place in a large bowl.

Beat the egg white in a separate bowl until fluffy, then beat in the salt and cornflour. Pour over the chicken and leave to stand for 15 minutes.

Heat a wok or frying pan and, when hot, add the oil. Heat for 30 seconds, then drain the chicken and add to the wok or frying pan and cook, stirring, for 2–3 minutes until sealed. Remove the chicken and reserve.

Add the carrots and peppers to the wok or frying pan and cook, stirring, for 3 minutes, or until the carrots have begun to soften. Stir in the curry paste and cook, stirring, for a further 2 minutes.

Add the stock, rice wine or vinegar, sugar and soy sauce. Stir well until blended, then return the chicken to the pan with the spring onions. Cook for 3–4 minutes until the chicken is thoroughly cooked. Serve with the sticky rice.

Chicken ❧ Ham Pie

Serves 4

1 tbsp olive oil
1 leek, trimmed and sliced
125 g/4 oz piece bacon,
cut into small dice
225 g/8 oz cooked boneless chicken
salt and freshly ground
black pepper
225 g/8 oz prepared
shortcrust pastry
plain flour, for dusting
2 medium eggs, beaten
150 ml/^{1}/$_4$ pint natural yogurt
4 tbsp chicken stock
1 tbsp poppy seeds

To serve:

sliced red onion
mixed salad leaves

Preheat the oven to 200°C/400°F/Gas Mark 6. Heat the oil in a frying pan and fry the leek and bacon for 4 minutes until soft but not coloured. Transfer to a bowl and reserve.

Cut the chicken into bite-size pieces and add to the leek and bacon. Season to taste with salt and pepper.

Roll out half the pastry on a lightly floured surface and use to line an 18 cm/7 inch, loose-based, deep flan tin. Scoop the chicken mixture into the pastry case.

Mix together 1 egg, the yogurt and the chicken stock. Pour the yogurt mixture over the chicken.

Roll out the remaining pastry on a lightly floured surface and cut out the lid to 5 mm/^{1}/$_4$ inch wider than the dish.

Brush the rim with the remaining beaten egg and lay the pastry lid on top, pressing the edges with the back of a knife to seal. Cut a hole in the centre to allow the steam to escape. Sprinkle with the poppy seeds and bake in the preheated oven for about 30 minutes until the pastry is golden brown. Serve with the onion and mixed salad leaves.

Turkey & Oven-roasted Vegetable Salad

Serves 4

4 tbsp olive oil
2 medium courgettes, trimmed and sliced
2 yellow peppers, deseeded and sliced
50 g/2 oz pine nuts (optional)
275 g/10 oz macaroni
350 g/12 oz cooked turkey
3 medium tomatoes, roughly chopped
2 tbsp freshly chopped coriander
1 garlic clove, peeled and chopped
3 tbsp balsamic vinegar
salt and freshly ground black pepper

Preheat the oven to 200°C/400°F/Gas Mark 6, 15 minutes before cooking. Line a large roasting tin with foil, pour in half the olive oil and place in the oven for 3 minutes, or until very hot. Remove from the oven, add the courgettes and peppers and stir until evenly coated. Bake for 30–35 minutes until slightly charred, turning occasionally.

Add the pine nuts, if using, to the tin. Return to the oven and cook for 10 minutes, or until the pine nuts are toasted. Remove from the oven and allow the vegetables to cool completely.

Bring a large pan of lightly salted water to a rolling boil. Add the macaroni and cook according to the packet instructions, or until *al dente*. Drain and refresh under cold running water, then drain thoroughly and place in a large salad bowl.

Cut the turkey into bite-size pieces and add to the macaroni. Add the tomatoes to the bowl with the cooled vegetables and pan juices. Blend together the coriander, garlic, remaining oil, vinegar and seasoning. Pour over the salad, toss lightly and serve.

Vegetables *and*

Vegetarian

Vegetables have been the inexpensive food option for centuries, which means there are endless delicious recipes to choose from. The selection provided here includes Italian dishes such as Sicilian Baked Aubergine and Vegetarian Spaghetti Bolognese as well as plenty of curries and savoury tarts. Even the pickiest of eaters will delight in this group of recipes!

Tagliatelle with Broccoli

Serves 4

450 g/1 lb broccoli, cut
into florets
125 g/4 oz baby corn
350 g/12 oz dried tagliatelle
2 tbsp dark soy sauce
1 tbsp dark muscovado sugar
1–2 tbsp white wine vinegar
1 tbsp sunflower oil
2 garlic cloves, peeled and finely
chopped
2.5 cm/1 inch piece fresh
root ginger, peeled and shredded
1 tsp dried chilli flakes,
or to taste
radish slices, to garnish

Bring a large saucepan of salted water to the boil and add the broccoli
and corn. Return the water to the boil, then remove the vegetables at
once using a slotted spoon, reserving the water. Plunge them into cold
water and drain well. Dry on kitchen paper and reserve.

Return the water to the boil. Add the tagliatelle and cook until *al dente*,
or according to the packet instructions. Drain well. Run under cold
water until cold, then drain well again.

Place the soy sauce, sugar and vinegar into a bowl. Mix well, then
reserve. Heat the oil in a wok or large frying pan over a high heat, add
the garlic, ginger and chilli flakes and stir-fry for about 30 seconds.
Add the broccoli and baby corn and continue to stir-fry for about
3 minutes.

Add the tagliatelle to the wok along with the soy sauce mixture and
stir together for a further 1–2 minutes until heated through. Season
to taste with salt and pepper. Garnish with the radish slices and
serve immediately.

Parsnip Tatin

Serves 4

1 quantity prepared shortcrust pastry
(*see* page 100 – or about
175 g/6 oz ready-made)
plain flour, for dusting

For the filling:

50 g/2 oz margarine or butter
8 small parsnips, peeled
and halved
1 tbsp brown sugar
75 ml/3 fl oz apple juice

Preheat the oven to 200°C/400°F/Gas Mark 6, 15 minutes before baking. Heat the margarine or butter in a 20.5 cm/8 inch frying pan.

Add the parsnips, arranging the cut side down with the narrow ends towards the centre. Sprinkle with sugar and cook for 15 minutes, turning halfway through, until golden.

Add the apple juice and bring to the boil. Remove the pan from the heat.

On a lightly floured surface, roll the pastry out to a size slightly larger than the frying pan. Position the pastry over the parsnips and press down slightly to enclose the parsnips.

Bake in the preheated oven for 20–25 minutes until the parsnips and pastry are golden. Invert a warmed serving plate over the pan and carefully turn the pan over to flip the tart onto the plate. Serve immediately.

Spinach & Mascarpone Pizza

Serves 4

1 quantity pizza dough
(*see* page 164)
plain flour, for dusting

For the topping:

3 tbsp olive oil
1 large red onion, peeled
and chopped
2 garlic cloves, peeled and
finely sliced
450 g/1 lb frozen spinach, thawed
and drained
salt and freshly ground
black pepper
3 tbsp tomato purée
125 g/4 oz mascarpone cheese
1 tbsp toasted pine
nuts (optional)

Preheat the oven to 220°C/425°F/Gas Mark 7, 15 minutes before baking. Knock the pizza dough with your fist a few times, shape and roll out thinly on a lightly floured board to form a 25 cm/ 10 inch round. Place on a lightly floured baking sheet and lift the edge to make a little rim. Place another baking sheet in the preheated oven to heat up.

Heat half the oil in a frying pan and gently fry the onion and garlic until soft and starting to change colour.

Squeeze out any excess water from the spinach and chop finely. Add to the onion and garlic with the remaining olive oil. Season to taste with salt and pepper.

Spread the tomato purée on the pizza dough and top with the spinach mixture. Mix the mascarpone with the pine nuts, if using, and dot over the pizza.

Slide the pizza onto the hot baking sheet and bake for 15–20 minutes. Transfer to a large plate and serve immediately.

Roasted Vegetable Pie

Serves 4

225 g/8 oz plain flour
pinch salt
50 g/2 oz white vegetable fat,
cut into cubes
50 g/2 oz butter, cut into cubes
2 tsp herbes de Provence
1 red pepper, deseeded
and halved
1 green pepper, deseeded
and halved
1 yellow pepper, deseeded
and halved
3 tbsp extra virgin olive oil
1 aubergine, trimmed and sliced
1 courgette, trimmed and
halved lengthways
1 leek, trimmed and
cut into chunks
1 medium egg, beaten
125 g/4 oz fresh mozzarella
cheese, sliced
salt and freshly ground black pepper
mixed herb sprigs, to garnish

Preheat the oven to 220°C/425°F/Gas Mark 7. Sift the flour and salt into a bowl, add the fats and mix lightly. Using the fingertips, rub into the flour until the mixture resembles breadcrumbs. Stir in the herbes de Provence. Sprinkle over a tablespoon cold water and, with a knife, start bringing the dough together (use your hands if necessary). If it does not form a ball instantly, add a little more water. Place in a polythene bag and chill for 30 minutes.

Place the peppers on a baking tray and sprinkle with 1 tablespoon of the oil. Roast for 20 minutes, or until the skins start to blacken. Brush the aubergine, courgette and leek with oil and place on another tray. Roast with the peppers for 20 minutes. Place the peppers in a polythene bag and leave the skins to loosen for 5 minutes. When cool, peel off the skins.

Roll out half the pastry on a floured surface and use to line a 20.5 cm/8 inch, round pie dish. Line with greaseproof paper and fill with baking beans, bake blind for about 10 minutes. Remove the beans and the paper, then brush the base with a little of the beaten egg. Return to the oven for 5 minutes. Layer the vegetables and the cheese in the pastry case, seasoning each layer. Roll out the remaining pastry on a floured surface and cut out a lid 5 mm/1/4 inch wider than the dish. Brush the rim with the egg, lay the lid on top and press to seal. Cut a slit in the lid and brush with the beaten egg. Bake for 30 minutes. Transfer to a large serving dish, garnish with sprigs of mixed herbs and serve immediately.

Creamy Vegetable Korma

Serves 4

2 tbsp vegetable oil
1 large onion, peeled and chopped
2 garlic cloves, peeled and crushed
1–2 tbsp korma curry powder or
paste, or to taste
finely grated zest and juice
of 1/2 lemon
50 g/2 oz ground almonds
400 ml/14 fl oz vegetable stock
450 g/1 lb potatoes, peeled
and diced
450 g/1 lb mixed vegetables, such
as cauliflower, carrots and turnip,
cut into chunks
125 ml/4 fl oz single cream
3 tbsp freshly chopped coriander
salt and freshly ground
black pepper
naan bread, to serve

Heat the oil in a large saucepan. Add the onion and cook for 5 minutes. Stir in the garlic and cook for a further 5 minutes, or until soft and just beginning to colour.

Stir in the curry powder or paste. Continue cooking over a low heat for 1 minute, stirring.

Stir in the lemon zest and juice and almonds. Blend in the vegetable stock. Slowly bring to the boil, stirring occasionally.

Add the potatoes and vegetables. Bring back to the boil, then reduce the heat, cover and simmer for 35–40 minutes until the vegetables are just tender. Check after 25 minutes and add a little more stock if needed.

Slowly stir in the cream and chopped coriander. Season to taste with salt and pepper. Cook very gently until heated through, but do not boil. Serve immediately with naan bread.

Aduki Bean ❧ Rice Burgers

Serves 4

2¹/₂ tbsp sunflower oil
1 medium onion, peeled and very
finely chopped
1 garlic clove, peeled and crushed
1–3 tsp curry paste, or to taste
225 g/8 oz basmati rice
400 g can aduki beans, drained
and rinsed
225 ml/8 fl oz vegetable stock
125 g/4 oz firm tofu, crumbled
2 tbsp freshly chopped coriander
salt and freshly ground
black pepper

For the carrot raita:

2 large carrots, peeled and grated
¹/₂ cucumber, cut into tiny dice
150 ml/¹/₄ pint Greek yogurt

To serve:

wholemeal baps
tomato slices
lettuce leaves

Heat 1 tablespoon of the oil in a saucepan and gently cook the onion for 10 minutes until soft. Add the garlic and curry paste and cook for a few more seconds. Stir in the rice and beans.

Pour in the stock, bring to the boil and simmer for 12 minutes, or until all the stock has been absorbed – do not lift the lid for the first 10 minutes of cooking. Reserve.

Lightly mash the tofu. Add to the rice mixture with the coriander, salt and pepper and mix.

Divide the mixture into four medium-size or eight small burgers. Chill in the refrigerator for 30 minutes.

Meanwhile, make the raita. Mix together the carrots, cucumber and Greek yogurt. Spoon into a small bowl and chill in the refrigerator until ready to serve.

Heat the remaining oil in a large frying pan. Fry the burgers, in batches if necessary, for 4–5 minutes on each side until lightly browned. Serve in the baps with tomato slices and lettuce. Accompany with the raita.

Mixed Grain Pilaf

Serves 4

2 tbsp olive oil
1 garlic clove, peeled and crushed
$^1/_2$ tsp ground turmeric
125 g/4 oz mixed long-grain
and wild rice
50 g/2 oz red lentils
300 ml/$^1/_2$ pint vegetable stock
200 g can chopped tomatoes
5 cm/2 inch cinnamon stick
salt and freshly ground
black pepper
400 g can mixed beans, drained
and rinsed

For the omelette:

15 g/$^1/_2$ oz margarine or butter
1 bunch spring onions, trimmed
and finely sliced
3 medium eggs
4 tbsp freshly chopped herbs,
such as parsley and chervil
fresh dill sprigs, to garnish

Heat 1 tablespoon of the oil in a saucepan. Add the garlic and turmeric and cook for a few seconds. Stir in the rice and lentils. Add the stock, tomatoes and cinnamon. Season to taste with salt and pepper. Stir once and bring to the boil. Lower the heat, cover and simmer for 20 minutes until most of the stock is absorbed and the rice and lentils are tender. Stir in the beans, replace the lid and leave to stand for 2–3 minutes to allow the beans to heat through.

While the rice is cooking, heat the remaining oil and the margarine or butter in a frying pan. Add the spring onions and cook for 4–5 minutes until soft. Lightly beat the eggs with 2 tablespoons of the herbs, then season with salt and pepper.

Pour the egg mixture over the spring onions. Stir gently with a spatula over a low heat, drawing the mixture from the sides to the centre as the omelette sets. When almost set, stop stirring and cook for about 30 seconds until golden underneath.

Remove the omelette from the pan, roll up and slice into thin strips. Fluff the rice up with a fork and remove the cinnamon stick. Spoon onto serving plates, top with strips of omelette and the remaining chopped herbs. Garnish with sprigs of dill and serve.

Layered Cheese & Herb Potato Cake

Serves 4

450 g/1 lb waxy potatoes
2 tbsp freshly snipped chives
1 tbsp freshly chopped parsley
125 g/4 oz mature Cheddar cheese
1 medium egg, beaten
1 tsp paprika
75 g/3 oz fresh white breadcrumbs
50 g/2 oz almonds, toasted and
roughly chopped
salt and freshly ground
black pepper
40 g/1¹/₂ oz margarine or
butter, melted
mixed salad or steamed vegetables,
to serve

Preheat the oven to 180°C/350°F/Gas Mark 4. Lightly oil and line the base of an 18 cm/7 inch round cake tin with greaseproof paper or baking parchment.

Peel and thinly slice the potatoes and reserve. Stir the chives, parsley, cheese and egg together in a small bowl and reserve. Mix the paprika into the breadcrumbs.

Sprinkle the almonds over the base of the lined tin. Cover with half the potatoes, arranging them in layers, then sprinkle with the paprika breadcrumb mixture and season to taste with salt and pepper. Spoon the cheese and herb mixture over the breadcrumbs with a little more seasoning, then arrange the remaining potatoes on top. Drizzle over the melted margarine or butter and press the surface down firmly.

Bake in the preheated oven for 1¹/₄ hours, or until golden and cooked through – check that the potatoes are tender all the way through by pushing a thin skewer through the centre. If the potatoes are still a little hard and the top is already brown enough, loosely cover with foil and continue cooking until done.

Let the tin stand for 10 minutes before carefully turning out and serving in thick wedges. Serve immediately with salad or freshly cooked vegetables.

Sicilian Baked Aubergine

Serves 4

2 aubergines, trimmed
2 tbsp olive oil
4 large, ripe tomatoes
2 celery stalks, trimmed
2 shallots, peeled and
finely chopped
1¹/₂ tsp tomato purée
25 g/1 oz pitted green olives
25 g/1 oz pitted black olives
salt and freshly ground
black pepper
1 tbsp white wine vinegar
2 tsp caster sugar
1 tbsp freshly chopped basil,
to garnish
mixed salad leaves, to serve

Preheat the oven to 200°C/400°F/Gas Mark 6, 15 minutes before baking. Cut the aubergines into small cubes and place on an oiled baking tray. Sprinkle with 1¹/₂ tablespoons of the oil.

Cover the tray with foil and bake in the preheated oven for 15–20 minutes until soft. Reserve to allow the aubergine to cool.

Using a sharp knife, score crosses in the tops of the tomatoes. Place the tomatoes and the celery in a large bowl and cover with boiling water. Remove the tomatoes from the bowl when their skins begin to peel away. Remove the skins, then deseed and chop the flesh into small pieces. Remove the celery from the bowl of water, chop finely and reserve.

Pour the remaining oil into a nonstick saucepan, add the chopped shallots and fry gently for 2–3 minutes until soft. Add the celery, tomatoes, tomato purée and olives. Season to taste with salt and pepper. Simmer gently for 3–4 minutes.

Add the vinegar, sugar and cooled aubergine to the pan and heat gently for 2–3 minutes until all the ingredients are well blended. Reserve to allow the aubergine mixture to cool. When cool, garnish with the chopped basil and serve cold with salad leaves.

Vegetarian Cassoulet

Serves 4

225 g/8 oz dried haricot beans,
soaked overnight
2 medium onions
1 bay leaf
1.5 litres/2 ^{1}/2 pints cold water
550 g/1 lb 3 oz large potatoes, peeled
and cut into 1 cm/^{1}/2 inch slices
5 tsp olive oil
1 large garlic clove, peeled
and crushed
2 leeks, trimmed and sliced
200 g/7 oz canned whole peeled
tomatoes, chopped
1 tsp dark muscovado sugar
1 tbsp freshly chopped thyme
2 tbsp freshly chopped parsley
salt and freshly ground black pepper
3 courgettes, trimmed and sliced

For the topping:
50 g/2 oz fresh white breadcrumbs
25 g/1 oz Cheddar cheese,
finely grated

Preheat the oven to 180˚C/350˚F/Gas Mark 4, 10 minutes before required. Drain the beans and rinse under cold running water, then place in a saucepan. Peel one of the onions and add to the beans with the bay leaf. Pour in the water. Bring to a rapid boil and cook for 10 minutes, then turn down the heat, cover and simmer for 50 minutes, or until the beans are almost tender. Drain the beans, reserving the liquor, but discarding the onion and bay leaf.

Cook the potatoes in a pan of lightly salted boiling water for 6–7 minutes until almost tender when tested with the point of a knife. Drain and reserve.

Peel and chop the remaining onion. Heat the oil in a frying pan and cook the onion, garlic and leeks for 10 minutes until softened. Stir in the tomatoes, sugar, thyme and parsley. Stir in the beans with 300 ml/ ^{1}/2 pint of the reserved liquor and season to taste. Simmer, uncovered, for 5 minutes.

Layer the potato slices, courgettes and ladlefuls of the bean mixture in a large casserole dish. To make the topping, mix together the breadcrumbs and cheese and sprinkle over the top. Bake in the preheated oven for 40 minutes, or until the vegetables are cooked through and the topping is golden. Serve.

Roasted Butternut Squash

Serves 4

2 small butternut squash
4 garlic cloves, peeled and crushed
2 tbsp olive oil
salt and freshly ground
black pepper
4 medium-size leeks, trimmed,
cleaned and thinly sliced
300 g can cannellini beans, drained
and rinsed
125 g/4 oz fine French beans, halved
1 tbsp wholegrain mustard, or
to taste
150 ml/¼ pint vegetable stock
50 g/2 oz rocket or watercress
2 tbsp freshly snipped chives
fresh chives, to garnish

To serve:

4 tbsp fromage frais
mixed salad

Preheat the oven to 200°C/400°F/Gas Mark 6, 15 minutes before roasting. Cut the butternut squash in half lengthways and scoop out all of the seeds.

Score the squash in a diamond pattern with a sharp knife. Mix the garlic with 1 tablespoon of the olive oil and brush over the cut surfaces of the squash. Season well with salt and pepper. Put on a baking sheet and roast for 40 minutes until tender.

Heat the remaining oil in a saucepan and fry the leeks for 5 minutes.

Add the drained cannellini beans, French beans, wholegrain mustard and vegetable stock. Bring to the boil and simmer gently for 5 minutes until the French beans are tender.

Remove from the heat and stir in the rocket or watercress and chives. Season well. Remove the squash from the oven and allow to cool for 5 minutes. Spoon in the bean mixture. Garnish with a few snipped chives and serve immediately with the fromage frais and a mixed salad.

Vegetarian Spaghetti Bolognese

Serves 4

2 tbsp olive oil
1 onion, peeled and finely chopped
1 carrot, peeled and finely chopped
1 celery stalk, trimmed and finely chopped
225 g/8 oz Quorn mince
450 ml/³/₄ pint vegetable stock
1 tsp mushroom ketchup (optional)
4 tbsp tomato purée
350 g/12 oz dried spaghetti
4 tbsp crème fraîche
salt and freshly ground black pepper
1 tbsp freshly chopped parsley

Heat the oil in a large saucepan and add the onion, carrot and celery. Cook gently for 10 minutes, adding a little water if necessary, until softened and starting to brown.

Add the Quorn mince and cook, stirring, for a further 2–3 minutes.

Mix together the vegetable stock and mushroom ketchup, if using, and add about half to the Quorn mixture along with the tomato purée. Cover and simmer gently for about 45 minutes, adding the remaining stock as necessary.

Meanwhile, bring a large pan of salted water to the boil and add the spaghetti. Cook until *al dente*, or according to the packet instructions. Drain well. Remove the sauce from the heat, add the crème fraîche and season to taste with salt and pepper. Stir in the parsley and serve immediately with the pasta.

Pumpkin & Chickpea Curry

Serves 4

1 tbsp vegetable oil
1 small onion, peeled and sliced
2 garlic cloves, peeled and finely chopped
2.5 cm/1 inch piece root ginger, peeled and grated
1 tsp ground coriander
$1/2$ tsp ground cumin
$1/2$ tsp ground turmeric
$1/4$ tsp ground cinnamon
2 tomatoes, chopped
2 red bird's-eye chillies, deseeded and finely chopped
450 g/1 lb pumpkin or butternut squash flesh, cubed
1 tbsp hot curry paste
300 ml/$1/2$ pint vegetable stock
1 large, firm banana
400 g can chickpeas, drained and rinsed, or 125 g/4 oz dried cannellini beans, soaked overnight
salt and freshly ground black pepper
1 tbsp freshly chopped coriander
coriander sprigs, to garnish
rice or naan bread, to serve

If using dried cannellini beans, drain and put into a saucepan with at least twice their volume of fresh water. Bring to the boil and boil rapidly for 10 minutes, then reduce the heat and simmer gently for a further 45–50 minutes until tender. Drain and reserve.

Heat the oil in a saucepan and add the onion. Fry gently for 5 minutes until softened. Add the garlic, ginger and spices and fry for a further minute. Add the chopped tomatoes and chillies and cook for another minute. Add the pumpkin and curry paste and fry gently for 3–4 minutes before adding the stock. Stir well, bring to the boil and simmer for 20 minutes until the pumpkin is tender.

Thickly slice the banana and add to the pumpkin, along with the chickpeas or cannellini beans. Simmer for a further 5 minutes.

Season to taste with salt and pepper and add the chopped coriander. Garnish with coriander sprigs and serve immediately with rice or naan bread.

Baby Onion Risotto

ℰ

Serves 4

For the baby onions:

1 tbsp olive oil
450 g/1 lb baby onions, peeled,
and halved if large
pinch sugar
1 tbsp freshly chopped thyme

For the risotto:

1 tbsp olive oil
1 small onion, peeled and
finely chopped
2 garlic cloves, peeled and
finely chopped
350 g/12 oz risotto rice
1.1 litres/2 pints vegetable
stock, heated
125 g/4 oz soft goats' cheese
salt and freshly ground
black pepper
fresh thyme sprigs, to garnish
rocket leaves, to serve

For the baby onions, heat the olive oil in a saucepan and add the onions with the sugar. Cover and cook over a low heat, stirring occasionally, for 20–25 minutes until caramelised. Uncover during the last 10 minutes of cooking.

Meanwhile, for the risotto, heat the oil in a large frying pan and add the onion. Cook over a medium heat for 5 minutes until softened. Add the garlic and cook for a further 30 seconds.

Add the risotto rice and stir well. Add the stock a ladleful at a time, stirring well and waiting until the last ladleful has been absorbed before stirring in the next. It will take 20–25 minutes to add all the stock, by which time the rice should be just cooked but still firm. Remove from the heat.

Add the thyme to the onions and cook briefly. Increase the heat and allow the onion mixture to bubble for a few minutes. Add the onion mixture to the risotto along with the goats' cheese. Stir well and season to taste with salt and pepper. Garnish with fresh thyme sprigs. Serve immediately with the rocket leaves.

Black Bean Chilli with Avocado Salsa

Serves 4

250 g/9 oz black beans or black-eye
beans, soaked overnight
2 tbsp olive oil
1 large onion, peeled and chopped
1 red pepper, deseeded and diced
2 garlic cloves, peeled and chopped
1 red chilli, deseeded and
finely chopped
2 tsp chilli powder
1 tsp ground cumin
2 tsp ground coriander
400 g can chopped tomatoes
450 ml/3/4 pint vegetable stock
1 small, ripe avocado, diced
1/2 small red onion, peeled and
finely chopped
2 tbsp freshly chopped coriander
juice of 1 lime
1 small tomato, peeled and diced
salt and freshly ground black pepper
25 g/1 oz dark chocolate
crème fraîche, lime slices and
coriander sprigs, to garnish

Drain the beans and place in a large saucepan with at least twice their volume of fresh water. Bring slowly to the boil, skimming off any froth that rises to the surface. Boil rapidly for 10 minutes, then reduce the heat and simmer for about 45 minutes, adding more water if necessary. Drain and reserve.

Heat the oil in a large saucepan and add the onion and pepper. Cook for 3–4 minutes until softened. Add the garlic and chilli. Cook for 5 minutes, or until the onion and pepper have softened. Add the chilli powder, cumin and coriander and cook for 30 seconds. Add the beans along with the tomatoes and stock. Bring to the boil and simmer uncovered for 40–45 minutes until the beans and vegetables are tender and the sauce has reduced.

Mix together the avocado, onion, fresh coriander, lime juice and tomato. Season with salt and pepper and set aside. Remove the chilli from the heat. Break the chocolate into pieces, or grate, if liked, and sprinkle over the chilli. Leave for 2 minutes. Stir well. Garnish with crème fraîche, lime slices and coriander. Serve with the avocado salsa.

Tomato ❧ Courgette Herb Tart

Serves 4

4 tbsp olive oil
1 onion, peeled and finely chopped
3 garlic cloves, peeled and crushed
400 g/14 oz prepared puff pastry,
thawed if frozen
plain flour, for dusting
1 small egg, beaten
2 tbsp freshly chopped rosemary
2 tbsp freshly chopped parsley
175 g/6 oz rindless, fresh, soft
goats' cheese
4 ripe plum tomatoes, sliced
1 medium courgette, trimmed
and sliced
thyme sprigs, to garnish

Preheat the oven to 230°C/450°F/Gas Mark 8, 15 minutes before baking.

Heat 2 tablespoons of the oil in a large frying pan. Fry the onion and garlic for about 4 minutes until softened and reserve.

Roll out the pastry on a lightly floured surface and cut out a 30 cm/12 inch circle. Brush the pastry with a little beaten egg, then prick all over with a fork. Transfer onto a dampened baking sheet and bake in the preheated oven for 10 minutes.

Turn the pastry over and brush with a little more egg. Bake for 5 more minutes, then remove from the oven.

Mix together the onion, garlic and herbs with the goats' cheese and spread over the pastry. Arrange the tomatoes and courgette over the goats' cheese and drizzle with the remaining oil. Bake for 20–25 minutes until the pastry is golden brown and the topping is bubbling. Garnish with the thyme sprigs and serve immediately.

Baking ❧ Desserts

These simple and delicious recipes will have you baking on a budget in no time. With savoury options such as Bacon & Tomato Breakfast Twist and Quick Brown Bread as well as tasty desserts such as Chocolate & Fruit Crumble and Raspberry Sorbet Crush, this section will provide you with the perfect finish to your wallet-friendly meals.

Quick Brown Bread

Makes two 450 g/1 lb loaves

700 g/1¹/₂ lb strong wholemeal flour
2 tsp salt
¹/₂ tsp caster sugar
7 g oz sachet fast-action dried yeast
450 ml/³/₄ pint warm water

To finish:

beaten egg, to glaze
1 tbsp plain white flour, to dust

For onion and caraway seed rolls:

1 small onion, peeled and
finely chopped
1 tbsp olive oil
2 tbsp caraway seeds
milk, to glaze

Preheat the oven to 200°C/400°F/Gas Mark 6, 15 minutes before baking. Oil two 450 g/1 lb loaf tins. Sift the flour, salt and sugar into a large bowl, adding the bran remaining in the sieve. Stir in the yeast, then make a well in the centre.

Pour the warm water into the dry ingredients and mix to form a soft dough, adding a little more water if needed. Knead on a lightly floured surface for 10 minutes, or until smooth and elastic. Divide in half, shape into two oblongs and place in the tins. Cover with oiled clingfilm and leave in a warm place for 40 minutes, or until risen to the tops of the tins.

Glaze one loaf with the beaten egg and dust the other loaf generously with the plain flour. Bake the loaves in the preheated oven for 35 minutes, or until well risen and lightly browned. Turn out of the tins and return to the oven for 5 minutes to crisp the sides. Cool on a wire rack.

For the onion and caraway seed rolls, gently fry the onion in the oil until soft. Reserve until the onion is cool, then stir into the dry ingredients with 1 tablespoon of the caraway seeds. Make the dough as before. Divide the dough into 16 pieces and shape into rolls. Put on two oiled baking trays, cover with oiled clingfilm and prove for 30 minutes. Glaze the rolls with milk and sprinkle with the rest of the seeds. Bake for 25–30 minutes, cool on a wire rack and serve.

Bacon Tomato Breakfast Twist

Serves 4

450 g/1 lb strong white flour
$^1/_2$ tsp salt
7 g sachet easy-blend dried yeast
300 ml/$^1/_2$ pint warm milk
15 g/$^1/_2$ oz margarine or butter, melted

For the filling:

225 g/8 oz back bacon, rind removed
15 g/$^1/_2$ oz margarine or butter, melted
175 g/6 oz ripe tomatoes, peeled, deseeded, chopped
freshly ground black pepper

To finish:

beaten egg, to glaze
2 tsp medium oatmeal

Preheat the oven to 200°C/400°F/Gas Mark 6, 15 minutes before baking. Sift the flour and salt into a large bowl. Stir in the yeast and make a well in the centre. Pour in the milk and margarine or butter and mix to a soft dough.

Knead on a lightly floured surface for 10 minutes until smooth and elastic. Put in an oiled bowl, cover with clingfilm and leave to rise in a warm place for 1 hour until doubled in size.

Cook the bacon under a hot grill for 5–6 minutes, turning once, until crisp. Leave to cool, then roughly chop.

Knead the dough again for a minute or two. Roll it out to a 25 x 33 cm/ 10 x 13 inch rectangle. Cut in half lengthways. Lightly brush with margarine or butter, then scatter with the bacon, tomatoes and black pepper, leaving a 1 cm/$^1/_2$ inch margin around the edges. Brush the edges of the dough with beaten egg, then roll up each rectangle lengthways.

Place the two rolls side by side and twist together, pinching the ends to seal. Transfer to an oiled baking sheet and loosely cover with oiled clingfilm. Leave to rise in a warm place for 30 minutes. Brush with the beaten egg and sprinkle with the oatmeal. Bake in the preheated oven for about 30 minutes until golden brown and hollow-sounding when tapped on the base. Serve the bread warm in thick slices.

Maple, Pecan & Lemon Loaf

Cuts into 12 slices

350 g/12 oz plain flour
1 tsp baking powder
175 g/6 oz margarine or
butter, cubed
75 g/3 oz caster sugar
125 g/4 oz pecan nuts,
roughly chopped
3 medium eggs
1 tbsp milk
finely grated zest of 1 lemon
5 tbsp maple syrup

For the icing:

75 g/3 oz icing sugar
1 tbsp lemon juice
25 g/1 oz pecans,
roughly chopped

Preheat the oven to 170°C/325°F/Gas Mark 3, 10 minutes before baking. Lightly oil and line the base of a 900 g/2 lb loaf tin with nonstick baking parchment.

Sift the flour and baking powder into a large bowl. Rub in the margarine or butter until the mixture resembles fine breadcrumbs. Stir in the caster sugar and pecan nuts.

Beat the eggs together with the milk and lemon zest. Stir in the maple syrup. Add to the dry ingredients and gently stir in until mixed thoroughly to make a soft dropping consistency.

Spoon the mixture into the prepared tin and level the top with the back of a spoon. Bake on the centre shelf of the preheated oven for 50–60 minutes until the cake is well risen and lightly browned. If a skewer inserted into the centre comes out clean, then the cake is ready.

Leave the cake in the tin for about 10 minutes, then turn out and leave to cool on a wire rack. Carefully remove the lining paper.

Sift the icing sugar into a small bowl and stir in the lemon juice to make a smooth icing. Drizzle the icing over the top of the loaf, then scatter with the chopped pecans. Leave to set, slice thickly and serve.

Carrot Cake

Cuts into 8 slices

200 g/7 oz plain flour
1/2 tsp ground cinnamon
1/2 tsp freshly grated nutmeg
1 tsp baking powder
1 tsp bicarbonate of soda
150 g/5 oz dark
muscovado sugar
200 ml/7 fl oz vegetable oil
3 medium eggs
225 g/8 oz carrots, peeled and
roughly grated
50 g/2 oz chopped walnuts

For the icing:

175 g/6 oz cream cheese
finely grated zest of 1 orange
1 tbsp orange juice
1 tsp vanilla extract
125 g/4 oz icing sugar

Preheat the oven to 150°C/300°F/Gas Mark 2, 10 minutes before baking. Lightly oil and line the base of a 15 cm/6 inch, deep, square cake tin with greaseproof paper or baking parchment.

Sift the flour, spices, baking powder and bicarbonate of soda together into a large bowl. Stir in the dark muscovado sugar and mix together.

Lightly whisk the oil and eggs together, then gradually stir into the flour and sugar mixture. Stir well. Add the carrots and walnuts. Mix thoroughly, then pour into the prepared cake tin. Bake in the preheated oven for 1 1/4 hours, or until light and springy to the touch and a skewer inserted into the centre of the cake comes out clean.

Remove from the oven and allow to cool in the tin for 5 minutes, then turn out onto a wire rack. Leave until cold.

To make the icing, beat together the cream cheese, orange zest, orange juice and vanilla extract. Sift the icing sugar and stir into the cream cheese mixture.

When the cake is cold, discard the lining paper, spread the cream cheese icing over the top of the cake and serve cut into squares.

Iced Bakewell Tart

Cuts into 8 slices

For the pastry:
175 g/6 oz plain flour
pinch salt
65 g/2¹/₂ oz margarine
or butter, cut into small pieces
50 g/2 oz white vegetable fat,
cut into small pieces
2 small egg yolks, beaten

For the filling:
125 g/4 oz margarine or
butter, melted
125 g/4 oz caster sugar
125 g/4 oz ground almonds
2 large eggs, beaten
few drops almond extract
2 tbsp seedless raspberry jam

For the icing:
125 g/4 oz icing sugar, sifted
6–8 tsp fresh lemon juice
25 g/1 oz toasted flaked almonds

Preheat the oven to 200°C/400°F/Gas Mark 6, 15 minutes before baking. Place the flour and salt in a bowl; rub in the margarine or butter and vegetable fat until the mixture resembles breadcrumbs. Alternatively, blend quickly, in short bursts, in a food processor.

Add the egg yolks, with sufficient water to make a soft, pliable dough. Knead lightly on a floured board, then chill in the refrigerator for about 30 minutes. Roll out the pastry and use to line a 23 cm/9 inch, loose-based flan tin.

For the filling, mix together the melted margarine or butter, sugar, almonds and beaten eggs and add a few drops almond extract. Spread the base of the pastry case with the raspberry jam and spoon over the egg mixture. Bake in the preheated oven for about 30 minutes until the filling is firm and golden brown. Remove from the oven and allow to cool completely.

When the tart is cold, make the icing by mixing together the icing sugar and lemon juice, a little at a time, until the icing is smooth and of a spreadable consistency. Spread the icing over the tart, leave to set for 2–3 minutes and sprinkle with the almonds. Chill in the refrigerator for about 10 minutes and serve.

Fruity Roulade

Serves 4

For the sponge:

3 medium eggs
75 g/3 oz caster sugar
75 g/3 oz plain flour, sifted
1–2 tbsp caster sugar, for sprinkling

For the filling:

125 g/4 oz Quark
125 g/4 oz Greek yogurt
25 g/1 oz caster sugar
1 tbsp orange liqueur (optional)
grated zest of 1 orange
125 g/4 oz strawberries, hulled and
cut into quarters

To decorate:

strawberries
icing sugar, sifted

Preheat the oven to 220˚C/425˚F/Gas Mark 7, 15 minutes before baking. Lightly oil and line a 33 x 23 cm/13 x 9 inch Swiss roll tin with greaseproof paper or baking parchment.

Using an electric whisk, whisk the eggs and sugar together until the mixture doubles in volume and leaves a trail across the top. Fold in the flour with a metal spoon or rubber spatula. Pour into the prepared tin and bake in the preheated oven for 10–12 minutes until ell risen and golden.

Place a whole sheet of greaseproof paper or baking parchment out on a flat work surface and sprinkle evenly with caster sugar. Turn the cooked sponge out onto the paper, discard the old paper, trim the sponge and roll up, encasing the paper inside. Reserve until cool.

To make the filling, mix together the Quark, yogurt, caster sugar, liqueur (if using) and orange zest. Unroll the roulade and spread over the mixture. Scatter over the strawberries and roll up.

Decorate the roulade with the strawberries. Dust with the icing sugar and serve.

Lemon Surprise

Serves 4

75 g/3 oz margarine or butter
175 g/6 oz caster sugar
3 medium eggs, separated
75 g/3 oz self-raising flour
450 ml/³⁄₄ pint milk
juice of 2 lemons
juice of 1 orange
2 tsp icing sugar
lemon twists, to decorate (optional)
sliced strawberries, to
serve (optional)

Preheat the oven to 190°C/375°F/Gas Mark 5. Lightly oil a deep, ovenproof dish.

Beat together the margarine or butter and sugar until pale and fluffy. Add the egg yolks, one at a time, with 1 tablespoon of the flour. Beat well after each addition. Once added, stir in the remaining flour. Stir in the milk, 4 tablespoons of the lemon juice and 3 tablespoons of the orange juice.

Whisk the egg whites until stiff and fold into the pudding mixture with a metal spoon or rubber spatula until well combined. Pour into the prepared dish.

Stand the dish in a roasting tin and pour in just enough boiling water to come halfway up the sides of the dish. Bake in the preheated oven for 45 minutes until well risen and spongy to the touch.

Remove the pudding from the oven and sprinkle with the icing sugar. If liked, decorate with the lemon twists and serve immediately with the strawberries.

Raspberry Sorbet Crush

Serves 4

225 g/8 oz raspberries, thawed
if frozen
grated zest and juice of 1 lime
300 ml/¹/₂ pint orange juice
225 g/8 oz caster sugar
2 medium egg whites

Set the freezer to rapid freeze. If using fresh raspberries, pick over and lightly rinse. Place the raspberries in a dish and, using a masher, mash to a chunky purée.

Place the lime zest and juice, orange juice and half the caster sugar in a large, heavy-based saucepan. Heat gently, stirring frequently, until the sugar has dissolved. Bring to the boil and boil rapidly for about 5 minutes.

Remove from the heat and pour carefully into a freezable container. Leave to cool, then place in the freezer and freeze for 2 hours, stirring occasionally to break up the ice crystals.

Fold the ice mixture into the raspberry purée with a metal spoon and freeze for a further 2 hours, stirring occasionally.

Whisk the egg whites until stiff, then gradually whisk in the remaining caster sugar a tablespoon at a time until the egg white mixture is stiff and glossy. Fold into the raspberry sorbet with a metal spoon and freeze for 1 hour. Spoon into tall glasses and serve immediately. Remember to return the freezer to its normal setting.

Gingerbread

175 g/6 oz margarine or butter
225 g/8 oz black treacle
50 g/2 oz dark muscovado sugar
350 g/12 oz plain flour
2 tsp ground ginger
150 ml/^{1}/$_4$ pint milk, warmed
2 medium eggs
1 tsp bicarbonate of soda
1 piece stem ginger in syrup
1 tbsp stem ginger syrup

Preheat the oven to 150°C/300°F/Gas Mark 2, 10 minutes before baking. Lightly oil and line the base of a 20.5 cm/8 inch, deep, round cake tin with greaseproof paper or baking parchment.

In a saucepan, gently heat the margarine or butter, black treacle and sugar together, stirring occasionally, until the butter melts. Leave to cool slightly.

Sift the flour and ground ginger into a large bowl. Make a well in the centre, then pour in the treacle mixture. Reserve 1 tablespoon of the milk, then pour the rest into the treacle mixture. Stir together lightly until mixed.

Beat the eggs together, then stir into the mixture.

Dissolve the bicarbonate of soda in the remaining 1 tablespoon warmed milk and add to the mixture. Beat until well mixed and free of lumps. Pour into the prepared tin and bake in the preheated oven for 1 hour, or until well risen and a skewer inserted into the centre comes out clean.

Cool in the tin, then remove. Slice the stem ginger into thin slivers and sprinkle over the cake. Drizzle with the syrup and serve.

Chocolate ✿ Fruit Crumble

Serves 4

For the crumble:

125 g/4 oz plain flour
125 g/4 oz margarine or butter
75 g/3 oz soft lightbrown sugar
50 g/2 oz rolled porridge oats
50 g/2 oz hazelnuts, chopped

For the filling:

450 g/1 lb Bramley apples
1 tbsp lemon juice
50 g/2 oz sultanas
50 g/2 oz seedless raisins
50 g/2 oz soft light brown sugar
350 g/12 oz pears, peeled, cored
and chopped
1 tsp ground cinnamon
125 g/4 oz plain dark chocolate,
very roughly chopped
2 tsp caster sugar, for sprinkling

Preheat the oven to 190°C/375°F/Gas Mark 5, 10 minutes before baking. Lightly oil an ovenproof dish.

For the crumble, sift the flour into a large bowl. Cut the margarine or butter into small dice and add to the flour. Rub the margarine or butter into the flour until the mixture resembles fine breadcrumbs. Stir the sugar, porridge oats and chopped hazelnuts into the mixture and reserve.

For the filling, peel the apples, core and thickly slice. Place in a large, heavy-based saucepan with the lemon juice and 3 tablespoons water. Add the sultanas, raisins and soft brown sugar. Bring slowly to the boil, cover and simmer over a gentle heat for 8–10 minutes, stirring occasionally, until the apples are slightly softened.

Remove the saucepan from the heat and leave to cool slightly before stirring in the pears, ground cinnamon and the chopped chocolate.

Spoon into the prepared ovenproof dish. Sprinkle the crumble evenly over the top, then bake in the preheated oven for 35–40 minutes until the top is golden. Remove from the oven, sprinkle with the caster sugar and serve immediately.

Index

Index